HUGH MCMILLAN was born in 1955 and lives in Penpont in Dumfries and Galloway. He is a poet and short story writer. He was the winner of the Smith Doorstep Poetry Competition in 2005, the Callum Macdonald Memorial Award in 2008, a winner in the Cardiff International Poetry Competition and was shortlisted for the Bridport Prize, the Michael Marks Award and the Basil Bunting Poetry Award in 2015. He is the recipient of five Arts Council or Creative Scotland bursaries and has been published, anthologised and broadcast widely in Scotland and abroad and translated into a variety of languages. An excellent reader of his own work, in recent years he has read to sell-out audiences at Wigtown Book Festival and Stanza Poetry Festival. He recently completed Wigtown Book Festival's first ever publishing commission on contemporary visions of Dumfries and Galloway. Luath Press will soon be publishing his latest book *McMillan's Galloway: A Creative Guide by an Unreliable Local.*

Not Actually Being in Dumfries

New and Selected Poems

HUGH McMILLAN

To Alison
all the Very Best
Hugh McMillan

Luath Press Limited
EDINBURGH
www.luath.co.uk

First published 2015
Reprinted 2016
Reprinted 2017

ISBN: 978-1-910745-10-6

The paper used in this book is recyclable. It is made from low
chlorine pulps produced in a low energy, low emissions manner
from renewable forests.

Printed and bound by
Bell & Bain Ltd., Glasgow

Typeset in 10.5 point Sabon by
3btype.com

Contents

from *Triumph of the Air*, 1989

from *Tramontana*, 1990

from *Horridge*, 1994

from *Aphrodite's Anorak*, 1996

from *After the Storm*, 2005

from *Strange Bamboo*, 2007

from *The Lost Garden*, 2010

Acknowledgements

Some of the uncollected poems here first appeared in *The Scotsman, The Herald, The Rialto, Northwords, The North, Gutter, Agenda, New Writing Scotland, Smith's Knoll, The Australian Journal of Poetry, Thin Slice of Moon* (Roncadora Press), *The Other Creatures in the Wood* (Mariscat) and *Scotia Nova* (Luath).

Previous collections comprise *Triumph of the Air*, Envoi Poets, 1989; *Tramontana*, Dog & Bone, 1990; *Horridge*, Chapman Publishing, 1994; *Aphrodite's Anorak*, Peterloo Poets, 1996; *After the Storm*, Smith/ Doorstop Books, 2005; *Strange Bamboo*, Shoestring Press, 2007; *The Lost Garden*, Roncadora Press, 2010.

Foreword

HUGH MCMILLAN is a poet's poet. He is also that other
rare thing, the author of several poems I wish I could
have written myself. I first became aware of his work in
the 1990s in the pages of the main Scottish literary
magazines of the day, such as *Chapman* and *Cencrastus*.
His satiric and witty poetic salvoes, with their
unexpectedly ironic turns and twists, beautifully capture
the place, the people and the character of his own
'locality', Dumfries and Galloway. I see in his poetry
some of my own aspiration to document in verse some
of my own locality's culture and history, through what
Tom Leonard calls 'ordinary discourse', which is of
course a feature of Scottish working-class oral poetry
that goes back beyond Burns to the Makars themselves.

If this all sounds a bit too bookish or 'worthy' then,
fear not, dear reader, for Hugh McMillan's subject is
neither William Dunbar nor the Kailyard but
contemporary Scotland, whose popular culture he
observes, breathes in, and registers in particularly vivid
fashion. From the vantage-point of a local bar, wild
cliff-top, history classroom or foreign holiday
destination, he fluently splices the particular with the
universal, which is the cultural legacy of all Scottish
poets since at least MacDiarmid, another Hugh,
another Borderer and another wanderer though
Scotland's literary, cultural and political 'identity' – but
thankfully without the doom-laden persona that his
namesake made into something like an art form,
although he had a lot to be pessimistic about.

Hugh McMillan is also a very 'personal' poet,
offering poems which openly reveal his love for his

family, his children, his lovers and friends often marbled through with an aching sense of absence, loss or abandonment that one senses is not simply related to the poem's 'persona' but intrinsic to the poet himself. Sometimes, the intimacy of his feelings are kept at bay or 'distanced' in certain poems by literary or historical references to ancient cultures or mythic figures, particularly Greek, which betray the extent to which this poet may not simply be the barstool philosopher he appears to be, but a genuinely erudite and geeky scholar. He also resembles MacDiarmid, a compulsive trawler-through of dictionaries and obscure manuscripts for nuggets of diamond intellectual clarity and brilliance, though MacDiarmid was an autodidact of the first order, not university-educated, like McMillan.

In this respect, Hugh often reminds me of Angus Calder, the radical literary scholar, poet and historian, whose 'Horace of Tollcross' persona revels in the howffs of Embro Old Town, a poet-scholar orchestrating in his own imagination an on-going conversation between the citizens and poets of ancient Athens and their counterparts in the Athens of the North. Try as he might to conceal it in his poetry, Hugh McMillan is as much a classicist as he is a family man or that fluent and articulate rat-arsed drunk at the end of the bar ranting about, well, almost anything one cares to mention. The proof is in these pages.

Finally, the best of the new generation of young poets writing in Scotland, Jen Hadfield, winner of the T.S.Eliot Prize, William Letford and Mandy Haggith, who all graduated through the Glasgow University Creative Writers course in recent years, remind me in their freshness, originality and daring of Hugh McMillan's work. If they have not already read it then they should, for there is much for anyone to savour and enjoy. Since Hugh McMillan's previous collections were produced by small independent publishers and some are no longer available, about a third of his previous output is included here. He remains in my opinion one of Scotland's foremost contemporary poetic voices. The proof is in these pages.

Alistair Findlay

Alistair Findlay is the author of *Shale Voices* (1999, 2010), a creative memoir of the shale-mining communities of West Lothian. He has written four collections of poetry, *Sex, Death & Football* (2003), *The Love Songs of John Knox* (2006), *Dancing With Big Eunice* (2010) and *Never Mind the Captions* (2011) and edited *100 Favourite Scottish Football Poems* (2007) and co-edited, with Tessa Ransford, *Scotia Nova: poems for the early days of a better nation* (2014)

Not Actually Being in Dumfries

When I am walking up Queensberry St in low cloud
and tread on chips floating in an oily puddle,
I am actually on the Cierro Del Sol, staring through trees
at ponds like pearl, the roses and myrtle.

When I turn onto the High Street at seven o'clock at night
and neds are stoned out of their brains and jeering,
I am hearing the sound of nightingales in gardens
with the heat still singing and the sun setting on fire.

At midnight I am not leaving the Hole in the Wa,
fumbling my way through a huddle of strange dwarves,
but moving statuesquely through the lush blooms
of my imagination, heavy and sweet as jacaranda,

and the night will not end here, in light to heavy drizzle,
and a taxi that fines you a hundred quid for being sick,
it will not end here in damp sandstone and shadows
but surely with a last long kiss below an orange moon.

Daydreams

I spend my day
by a narrow window.
There's cloud like mist,
a meticulously tiled roof,
a gull about to step off
into the unseen
dizziness of space.

Through the window
are other windows, too,
and behind them people
swim mysteriously
back and forth,
as though butting the sides
of a bowl.

When I tire of watching this,
I turn to things I wish
would happen.
Light is photons
flying through the air like birds,
after all,
blazing as dreams.

Is it possible
to step through the glass
into the air
like the gull,
into the dream?

Notebook

I'm about to bin a notebook,
a lost stocking filler,
wrinkled by damp and empty,
though I see parts were used,
one summer, years before.

There's my wife's writing,
small, angled as cuneiform,
estimates for laminate flooring
and a note to a heating engineer,
'What is the boiler's life expectancy?'

and here's a poem I recognise,
sprawled new born and needy on the page.
The girls have the centre spread, of course,
a river swirling through forest
with wading unicorns and fish.

The poet, the home-maker, the little dreamers:
read like that you miss what's empty and unsaid;
the dreams of the homemaker;
the calculations of the poet;
the other creatures in the wood.

Hoagies

When there's traffic in my mind,
I end up in Philadelphia,
strolling in the Avenue of the Arts
with a well-groomed girl,
or punching the air like Rocky
on the steps of the Rodin Museum
at the sight of another by-line
from Scoop McMillan.
As I eat hoagies in the
unusually mild weather this Fall,
I watch leaves slowly drift to sea.
At this point I'm interrupted by a bum.
What is a hoagie? he asks.
And what's it like to be on the edge
of a humid subtropical zone?
He's drunk again, and on Wikipedia,
and soon he'll show me, irresistibly,
pictures of his home town.

A Gift, after the Event

In the photograph you kindly sent me
I am wading in the Acheron.
I do not look perturbed,
though trees trail on water
and drowned leaves point
between cliffs to the land of the dead.
I am going cheerily down, it seems,
in unlikely denim shorts and a back-pack,
a smile on my face. Perhaps I am thinking
of the Fields of Asphodel
where souls comically circle like bats,
but more likely I am anticipating
a pint and a Greek Salad, certainly
not the drama to come.
If I'd known I was near to the brink,
I would have paid attention.
'You, on your way to Hell',
added thoughtfully, in black biro.

Twelfth Night

All the needles are hoovered,
the decorations that the paper chain gang
slaved to put in place pulled down,
and the festivity, all the hoo-hah,
is gone in a few seconds, pffff,
the walls and floor and ceiling
cold and clean as January again.
Later, the kids look for evidence,
glitter below the settee maybe,
or a crumb of carrot the reindeer left,
why do *they* need proof the whole
thing was not, after all, a dream?
The wreath, they shout, and run to see,
but the door is bare, only light rain on it,
and they settle into life again,
the prospect of birthdays, holidays to come,
and then there's only me,
staring at another arthritically curled tree
wondering whether to save that thread of tinsel
burning in the evening streetlight,
one last ember still in the heart of the pine.

Silences

When the girls have gone I think
once that dove has cleared the fence
like a plane on one propeller,
there will be silence and the weather at last to enjoy it
but soon I'm listening to a blackbird crooning
and behind that there are insects
and a stir of breeze in these leaves too
which amounts to the smallest of sounds,
but there's something else,
a wash of traffic maybe
or pebbles far away in the sea shifting
in their tide of perfect blue,
or is it a small tree growing bark?
Or is it the sound at the very core of the world
that holds unlikely things together,
like glue, or longing?

Book Launch, Oxford 2009

Tasha is just out of poets' school,
where she was Head Girl,
and Bridget and Dan have the same hat.
They say I'm authentic
but I'm merely filthy drunk
and hanging about the refreshments
because if the Merlot's run out already
there's going to be trouble.
I read last, as the rest have somewhere to go,
and because there's swearing in mine.
What do they think I am, a token Scotsman,
some kind of caricature?
I give a small, angry stagger.
Isn't it odd, I say to a total stranger,
the number of Scottish drunks
in TV Drama? Outraged, I spend
the rest of the night
teaching a woman in a wheelchair
the right way you say get tae fuck.

The Visitation: Jacob Epstein

She stands
on tip toe,
in a clasp of trees,
hair neatly plaited,
hands folded,
her face pushed forward
into mine as if
I was the voice,
I was the spirit
rehearsing the words
for those straining ears,
'chosen among women'.
But not me,
oh no little Mary,
not me.

My Father from Extant Sources

The Oral Tradition
He was a bad bastard, well shot of him.

The Pictorial Evidence
He and his brother sat greasy haired on a gate,
their faces full of something worse than mischief:
Fat Boab and Soapy Soutar, grown bad in Auchinleck.
Another, on a horse, tanned and short sleeved,
watching the desert flatten to white waves.
Lawrence of Dumfries.

Moving Images
Mack Sennett outtakes spliced together
and replayed so often in the Multiplex of my head
that every detail's dodgy. Did he really jump that river
from a standing start? Did he really talk to the dead?

The Written Sources
Assorted documents confirming
he was the son and grandson of pitmen,
some Masonic certificates, well thumbed,
a 40s sex manual, mint condition,
a short story, unfinished, about men
who didn't know they'd been killed at Alamein,
and a short account, unsigned, of his funeral
and a grave somewhere near Fortingall.

Other
That painting he left in the attic, a tree
dissected against a nightmare's sky,
with a thumb-print sunk in oils like a caldera,
the centre of a brief but violent storm.

The Day of Willie Neill's Funeral

The trees were pale and bare
like fossils framed in mud,
the sun a pulse in water.
The day eked out, long,
thin as old skin
or air too high in the hills.

I held a cord:
he wasn't heavy to my hands.
A piper played
though it was fair to say
the blackbird was better.
At funerals the poets

grow more bald and scared
of death. They eat lunch
and leave, anxious
to court life again.
I was not ashamed
to cry, not for the Makar,

too spent for tears,
the bleed of years.

Saturday Morning

Across the water on the Greensands,
two early morning drunks are fighting,
rolling over cut grass like lovers.
Here, balanced sturdily on a railing,
is a seagull, eyes cold as a Viking's.
It is desperate for a crust
that's nestled snug
in the dirt below this bench.
What brings us to these depths,
misfits from two noble species,
our holy grails pale things
made from flesh or pizza dough?
We will not be deterred,
not by this fine rain, nor instincts
of when the world was fresh
and the sun a diamond cut in space.
We watch each other,
it is a waiting game, decline,
and the river makes its usual
slow
horrified
way to sea.

My Parents' Marriage

The chair left patterns on my bare legs
but the Moffat House Hotel
was the height of sophistication.
Every Saturday we sat in total silence,
drank tea, speared little cakes with forks.
All through autumn 1963,
as rain drummed on windows,
in a room lined with wood like a coffin:
cake after cake after cake.

Excavation

Emptying cupboards from
the pre-Homeric Classroom era,
through strata thick as Schliemann's Troy.
I am looking for bedrock and
the world before printing
when we worked with our bare minds
or a single piece of paper rolled
soaking wet from a banda machine.
When times were tough, we drank the fluid
and went outside to fight hairy colleagues from other lands.
Who can forget 1978 when that probationer
stole the Headmaster's wife
and we sailed across the Firth in a fleet of long keeled ships,
the sun glinting on our oars?
Our beards have grown, our blood coarsened,
paper has closed over our bones like sand.
But there is a hot deep wind today at the skip.
It takes the sheets and spins them over rooftops,
all the dense tyrannies of words
gone to air at the end, like birds.

Grounded

I do not remember my father's big hands fondly,
but years have passed
and memory rots like old film
and what was my terror to his,
in that glass cube
with the howl of engines
and the voices of the others in his ears shrill as birds?
Each night he scoured the folds of dark for death.

'Corkscrew port' he'd shout,
'Corkscrew port!'
Both of us would shrink, shut up,
but he'd let rip,
a long burst from the brownings
in his head I see now.
How could we know it was the smallest
quietest things he feared the most?

Caedmon Singing in his Barn

I did not mean to describe you
as loony looking, but lovely.
I can't tell you this because
my phone has turned against me,
as if the odds were not heavy enough
this winter, with these moods
and my growing decrepitude.
I would write a letter
but in spite of loving you for years
I don't know the address.
My HTC Desire can tell me
your nearest mast and the hours
of daylight you had today
and the knowledge pleases,
but the end of a trail of impulses
is where you've always been for me:
I've imagined it like a path overgrown
but straight as an arrow to my heart.
It's impossible to explain,
my feelings filtered at the end into Frisian,
like Caedmon singing in his barn, in a dream,
alone and full of love, *scharen vie losung yon.*

My Sister Went to Guayaquil

Guayaquil,
to hear my mother,
was the whorehouse
at the end of the universe,
the frontier town you see
in films, with stubbled men
and showgirls and nightly
shoot-outs in the street.
'Gone to Guayaquil'
was mother-speak
for gone to fuck,
beyond all sense and morality.

I on the other hand
thought it good you'd gone
to Guayaquil, imagined
you sipping daiquiris
in the colonnaded shade
of an ex-colonial house
while the ocean shone
silver to the horizon.
Imagine my surprise then,
when you came back
with that strange tattoo,
and pregnant, and told her
she was absolutely right.

The Workshop Exercise is 'Write about a Potato'

When I think about a potato
I don't think about mountains
capped in cloud or lochs
like clasps that hold the sun
or birds scratching the surface
of the sea's dark eye
somewhere near Mull,
land where I have never
grown potatoes.

A potato is not what comes to my mind
when I think of my love,
or the laughter of my kids
as they run into the distance
in a dizzy dream of light,
and that tall glass of beer
I am working towards
with all this creative fervour
is nothing like a potato.

I don't want to get personal,
but to me the poet organizing this
looks more and more like a potato,
but there's no poem there,
so in the febrile landscape of life,
its agonies, its bliss
and hopeless cruelties,
we must carry on rooting
amongst the potatoes.

Starcat

Every Saturday morning
we meet, my daughter and I,
to study form. She has a plain scone,
sometimes an empire biscuit,
I have coffee. I used to have an egg roll
but she didn't like the way it ran
yellow onto the napkin.
After a moment or two she'll
put on her latest pair of glasses
give a slight frown and get to it.
Stars are good, Elektra Star, Mystery Star,
but cats are best, Kenya Cat, Lightning Cat,
Son of Cat. How the pair of us rejoiced
when Starcat was on the card at Ascot,
an alchemy just for us it seemed,
a totemic and irresistible blend
of the cosmic and the cute.
Stars are usually eighth, cats more spry
but still well down the field.
Starcat lost, its life in fact.
I say it has retired and today is eating grass
in the verdant field of our imagining,
a place where people of different ages
often come, to watch horses take wing,
and two bob make a thousand quid.

Hugelshofer, Jackson, Gilruth, Chinnock and Bain

A black and white photograph:
It would be a brave colour
that would infiltrate this group,
sat gowned and booted
outside the school in 1913.
They stare at the camera
their mortar boards in unbroken line.
I see it's sunny, from shadow
and the light like a mortar bomb
bursting through trees behind,
perhaps the end of summer term.

Chinnock is the headmaster
by virtue of his moustache which is bigger
than the sum of the square
of the other two moustaches.
It is a comical moustache though you sense
you would not say this near Chinnock.
Bain does not have a moustache,
she is a woman, and has caused
a small seismic stir in the seating,
you can see it rippling away still.

Jackson to her left
has pulled some distance away
back towards the Paleozoic era
when women knew they were fish.
Gilruth is the joker of the group,
hat askew, he wears a quizzical look.
His hand is on a chain that dangles
from the deep folds of his jacket.
Perhaps he is thinking if he pulls it,
Chinnock will be ejected into the undergrowth,
Then he could sit next at last to Bain,
remove the flowerpot from her head,
and declare his love.

Hugelshofer. Not even port
in the Headmaster's study
will cheer him up this year.
He knows
the strapping lads he coached this morning
in Catullus
are marked for death.

Letter

Here is a letter
come across the membrane of ocean
over the back of a world
curved like a whale.
I unwrap it, like tissue,
and sentences spill out,
as though the seal on a jar has broken,
coils of cornflower blue
on paper thin as shell.

I saw a sailor's valentine once
in a museum in Nantucket Sound,
a mosaic of broken scallop
glued in a compass rose.
'Writ from the heart' it said.
Words come best like that:
in ink or blood,
when the source is from a major vein.

I read, and understand this much:
if ink sees off time and miles, then so must love.

Too Big a Part

Last night the girls got their parts in the nativity.
Lydia is reprising last season's triumph as the
Angel of Glory, all blondeness and glitter
looming like a valkyrie over star-struck shepherds.
Jasmine is to be Mary and distraught
to be pushed into the big time so soon.
We try to reassure her. Mary is the easiest,
we say, she doesn't speak, all she does is follow Joseph
and stand around with a baby. There's sheep, we say,
and you get to ride the donkey, but to no avail.
Jasmine stands at the window, tears mirrored
in the fat glass, as unsure of her place in the very centre
of the puzzle as presumably that woman was then,
        turning
in her palm over and over, the luck of the world.

The End of the Holidays

The bay is flat
and the islands like stones on it.
We are trying to have a quiet drink,
there are things I need to say,
but you phone your friend Steve
to see if he's ok and turns out
he's in a tree in Salford
about to hang himself,
with someone called Pete,
a traffic engineer, trying to
talk him down.
I order and we sit
at a scarred wooden table.
The bar is empty, in the corner
a fruit machine winks spasmodically.
Steve you are saying, Steve, listen
nothing is as bad as it seems.
I take a mouthful.
Through the high window
gulls are circling slowly
in a sky like paste.
Steve, you can't hang yourself
at Christmas, think of the kids.
I take another, and the beer
washes over the smooth surface
of the glass leaving flecks
of foam like the sea.
Pete is that you? Are you in the tree?

The beermat says there are nearly 800 islands
off the coast of Scotland.
You put the phone down for a moment,
to find a tissue with which to wipe your eyes
and in the distance I'm sure I hear
the cops arriving.

Flacking Crombled wi' Dwank Shommers o Drod an Fistering Sleugh

In the language of this remote area there are many terms for the feeling you get when you see –

a grey mist creeping down a cold hill
where some wet sheep are waiting stoically

flacking crombled wi dwank shommers o drod an
    fistering sleugh

* * *

Drod (n) Dull, indefinable feeling prefiguring one's own
    death
Sleugh (n) Psychosomatic, but terrifyingly real, sense of
    nausea
Fister (v) To creep sickeningly slowly like an injured beast
Shommers (n) imagined things that seem very real
Dwank (adj) (archaic) Black, sodden, wet, often a carcass
Flacking (adj) Too weak to move while simultaneously
    exasperated
Crombled (adj) Crippled, hunched, as if by great age or
    boredom

Reborn

George Dickie didn't hack it as a butcher,
swapped the blood and offal
for a uniform, and when its shade didn't suit him,
vanished in London among the dispossessed:
the distaste back home was palpable.
Then George Dickie became Jack Brent,
and took a bullet in the spine
for the poor at Jarama,
limped back, battling still for the flag
red as carnations,
as the blood of Spain.
On the sodden streets of Whithorn now,
there's a splash of colour and a communist star:
'Un heroe de la guerra civil de espanola'.
How disgusting some said,
so close to a shrine of Christ
who gave his life and was reborn to save us all.

Your Boyfriend Was A Red

I remember my father
squaring up to your boyfriend
when he said hurrah for
the Provisional IRA.
Even in short trousers
I knew how terrible this was,
though I admired how,
unlike my father,
your boyfriend was seven feet tall
with a full head of hair,
and a beard like some ancient warrior's.
I liked too that he waited
until after dessert
to insult our nation's dead.
Looking back at it now though,
the thing I recall with most happiness
is how, in the late autumn sunlight
of that car park, my fathers
bald head bobbed and waggled
frantically, shining, ironically,
a bright shade of red.

Landing in Neapolis

Like one of Homer's ships
beached on the bone white sand,
not sand at all but a million
shells holding the keel tight.
Imagine men leaping into the light

and arrows like a fine rain
on the cliffs ahead.
But there are only neat tables here
under the shade of pine and jasmine,
some lobster pots on a broken pier

and a lorry grunting
away through shimmer.
In the town I left,
bollards stand along the river
and ships exist in photographs

or the names of pubs,
sluggish water winds
towards the ocean
but only pizza boxes make it
further than the silt.

Just a crust of the past is left
anywhere, the faintest trace.
I can't imagine the life
of the person next to me,
never mind folk a thousand years ago.

Summerisle

What has happened here?
Why are the cottages shuttered,
the streets primed for tumbleweed?
Where are the zimmers,
the folk carrying parcels of fish,
the kids drumming on fences,
the men and women walking back
leaden footed from work?
Only the offices to prevent
rural depopulation are open,
their computer screens flickering
madly behind half closed blinds.
I am waiting for these small villages
by the sea to regenerate,
like in some film,
to be born of flame,
and while I do, public art sprouts
above me,
huge and mysterious like alien seed.

Eating Seafood

February, all light is bulbs or wrung through clouds
like grey underwear, the sun is bright lemon
only in drawings stuck to the brick.
Where are you as I stare at this plastic tablecloth
counting the white dots that blur like snow on a field?
You are eating seafood, of course,
in some bar or restaurant, or in your warm kitchen.
You are always eating seafood; in my mind
the scene is delicately shaded, with pearly overtones,
like Renoir's 'Girl Always Eating Seafood'.
Of the many things I may not have with you
why is seafood the most affecting?
Perhaps that answer is within reach,
like the dots, like taupe, a colour I didn't know existed
till today, and can't pronounce. Such things I find!
There are 46 dots, I ticked each off in pencil,
just before death became preferable.

Tales of the Treehouse

I am talking to my children
on the phone about parrots.
In Scotland it is raining,
the kind of drizzle
I bet that is like a layer of skin.
Here, I say,
the parrots are drunk
in the bottlebrush trees.
Here, I don't say,
the poet is drunk below
the bottlebrush trees,
striped in sunshine
below the lighthouse
that gleams like a strange tooth,
whose beam at night
crosses the skies,
the hearts,
of the dreamers,
the drunks, the lovers.

End of Year Exam

A floorboard creaks
but mostly it's like the sea,
old grain flowing like dark water.
Overhead, through tall windows,
the breeze catches clouds.
It is a voyage this, just the beginning,
but they are moving away,
sails are filling,
they are beating time on paper with ink,
the destination a dream,
the impetus all that matters,
the keel dragging free of shale.

Jock Tamson's Beach Bar

That engine, so low and distant,
takes me back to Newhaven,
the foghorns across the Forth
and Fife out there somewhere
in a starless night.
Scottish seas make you sad:
the one on the right
with its squalls and black ice;
the one on the left that rubs
on empty islands and sounds
when its dark like a song;
even the one down the bottom corner,
a runt of a sea
with its mud creeks and rotten jetties
and sly looks at England.
It's not like that here,
the waves spark and fizz like electricity,
a perfect bowl of blue that seals the eyes.
Aphrodite came out of these waters,
bringing love,
what came out of ours?
Grey ships, going everywhere.

Reading Billy Collins in the Bath

I am reading you in the bath
and you are doing that thing again,
making me want to laugh then strangle you,
not just because the little factual paragraph
on the typeface in your perfect book
is better than most poems I write,
nor because, thanks to a CD I bought,
I hear your lugubrious voice sounding
every syllable like a soft and distant bell,
but mostly because after a few pages,
the mundane in the bathroom, and in all
the rooms in this old house, begins to resonate
like some small but perfect oriental poem.
For instance, my wife just came in
and as she spoke about lunch
a sudden lick of sunshine fell across
her face like a dazzling Arab veil.
I am wishing for a squadron of tanks
to knock the village down, or an aircraft
to fall from the sky like a bird arrowed
at the breast, so I can say
'Stick that in your pipe Billy Collins',
but I suppose even from such an event,
tender gold would be spun like thread
at the end of day, birds would sing a tattoo,
and those still alive beyond
the immediate wreckage area of these
imaginary catastrophes would look up
at their stars, and go quietly to sleep.

The Balcony of the Salutation Hotel

There's a balcony in Dumfries,
between willows,
above the black wall of river,
and when the sun's hung above it,
no doubt at all it's Venice,
and from Venice isn't it just a step,
when the light falls on water
like shining pieces of a mirror,
to happiness?
It's nothing like Venice, you say,
when you're up there it's freezing
and unsafe,
but so is dreaming
and there are rats,
rats too, in Venice and in dreaming.
The thing is, you're thinking
of the Venice in that lagoon,
at the top of the Adriatic,
not the one in my brain where,
lit by electrical impulses
like the Lido at night from Sant'Elena,
we can have love and poetry all year long.

Another Day in South West Scotland

I lost it today,
rounded on an old couple
in the discreetly pine panelled reception room
of the Buccleuch and Queensberry Arms Hotel.
It was as though I had never heard
how to politely debate
with adversaries and point them,
using diplomacy and charm,
to an alternative point of view.
Instead, I'm afraid, I offered
to ram the rolled up copy
of the *Daily Mail* they were brandishing
up their arses, one pensioner at a time.
There was a silence then.

Then minutes later on the Nith,
a deer was breasting the water
in a sudden blaze of sun like gold.
There should have been a soundtrack,
and there was, in my head,
a rage for my weans to see
good things, be good things,
to stand apart from mediocrity,
arrogance and lies,
and I'm standing just across that bridge now,
willing the little tiger-stripe of sun to follow,
to feel it on my back, like the deer,
breaking from trees into light.

Auchencairn, and Scotland, as it Might Be

Dick Hattaraik and Billy Marshall
are drinking at the bar.
It's blue and carved from a boat
and they are sharing some porky scratchings
smuggled over last night from Holland.
On the bay, the Black Pearl, no Prince,
rocks at anchor, carronades trained
steadily up the Dumfries road.
Outside, in a blaze of grass and yellow vetch,
some of Billy's hundred and twenty children
play with an exciseman's hat,
while the exciseman himself
sits blushing, winding yarn for the daughter
whose beauty like Helen of Troy's
is renowned from coast to coast.
It is June, the start of a brilliant summer,
they are breathing the air of Galloway
and it is rich in love and brandy and revolution.
Boundaries shimmer, shift like haze.
It's mathematically possible, in fact,
for Burns to come in
and put the icing on the cake.
Should I speak?
Tell my tales of a bit of baccy
smuggled in euro lorries,
the angry letters I've written to *The Standard*,
my hidden fear that in an independent Scotland
my pension might suffer?
Maybe not.

Another Day in South West Scotland 2

Grey sky breaks into streaks of blue.
Now if I was King Oenghus en route
to gub the English at Nechtansmere
I would see a metaphor there,
but instead I am alone
on a rain swept street of sandstone,
pushing leaflets through doors
for faceless terriers to chew.
There is a single cottage over there,
where someone has erected
a wooden sign with yes painted gold.
I sit on the wall,
as if this was the Scottish Embassy
in some foreign country.
Inside I imagine an office with a tartan carpet
and walls tastefully decorated
with pictures of the Kelpies
and the Star of Caledonia
where a pretty red-haired girl at a desk
is refusing to give me pounds or merks
to keep me going till the next plane
to Burns International,
explaining patiently, but insistently,
that I don't need repatriation,
because I am, unbelievably, home.

Fairies

The moon is a dull blade
and everything beyond
the pond of street lamp
is gone except two blue lights
swimming: maybe a house in the hills
or a 737 coming home to Glasgow,
or then again fairies.
It doesn't look more
than half a mile,
worth the soaking,
when I burst into the circle
and they slowly turn
their hard little faces to me
white and beautiful
in the light,
like dolls.

The Flight of the Techno-Quarks

I awake to news that the thousand
scientists who have been trying
for years to find the 'God particle'
may have discovered "something else".
They do not say what:
perhaps it is a pound of mince,
a small grandmother knitting in her kitchen,
or the source of love.
No, they announce finally,
it is techni-quarks.
I sense disappointment in their voices.
Maybe God is weeping too,
from relief, but it is the techni-quarks
I feel sorry for,
bound together in the cold tunnels
of Switzerland, continually pummelled
by the Large Hadron Collider,
haunted by dreams of anti-matter.
Science can be so cruel.
In my mind's eye I see the techni-quarks
free, flying south for the winter,
landing in a flock at the sea's edge
and turning small invisible
faces to the sun.

Caroline Herschel's Christmas

They pitied Caroline Herschel,
marked by typhus,
but while other girls picked goose bones,
dreamed of kissing-boughs,
she was in the garden
with a 2.2 Newtonian Telescope
pointing at the northern part of Monoceros
on the midpoint of a line
from Procyon to Betelgeuse,
where the ionised hydrogen forms
a haze of stars
that emerge from leaves of sky
like pearls.
When they wondered if she might
be tempted inside
for pudding, some society,
she demurred,
preferring instead
to watch the birth of light.

I see White Birds Walk on Ice

The phone shakes
with the message of another death,
a man caught in mid anecdote
by a haemorrhage,
and not a drop of lager spilled.

I am counting the trees
on Ward Law, tall pines
that pierce the sky:
it is winter, as always;
birds move on glazed fields.

A thing that worries me
disproportionately
is what will happen
to the little bits of paper
in my pockets,

will someone read them
and weep at the detritus
of a futile life,
or foolishly try to cash
in the slip for Shotavodka

a horse still running
through the fog at Kempton?
So much stuff to lug around,
arteries, return tickets to Gatehouse,
and all slowly running out.

Settlement

I spend a lot of time in the hills
but there are always sheep above me,
hanging in space on their stilt legs,
or at the very edge of my vision
circling crags like small clouds.

When the mountains crumble
into the new age of seas,
they will survive,
they will bump along the ocean floor
with blank expressions

chewing seaweed,
their lambs coming and going
quickly, like fish.
It will be a mystery how this will happen
but it will:

those with a bit of brain,
seeing the absurdity of their situation,
will drown, but the vast crowd,
having no doubts of their own,
will take it as read.

The Black Loch

We climb the track, and go
through the ghost of gardens,
seats melted to moss,
a stone heron by a pond
lacquered with shorewood.

There's a gap in the wall,
and a bluebell path
cut by the edge of a burn,
but we leave fairyland
for wilder stuff, where pines
brood on hilltops and each
step slips on centuries.

At last through the trees,
a skin of water rippling with fire,
ancient as the forest,
the Black Loch,
as old maybe as the rock tombs
bound in bracken at its side.

Here people of the parish
left gifts as their fathers had,
took the cold spring water,
while the Minister fumed
in his pulpit far below.
There's no-one now,
nor trace there ever was,
as we look at the surface,
flat as glass except for the tiny
needling of dragonflies,
as we listen to the silence
behind the song of lovesick birds.

from *Triumph of the Air*, 1989

Triumph of the Air

I didn't know what gliding was
but I liked it:
while my father juggled hot geysers of air
high above the patchwork frazzle of Edinburgh,
I was left at my Gran's,
in a carpet like the ocean,
butting through squalls of wool and lavender,
past mahogany islands,
harvests of anemones,
to the edge of the world
where doors boomed like cliffs
and continents of furniture tapered away
to snowfields of china cups,
and dust swam in helesponts of light, blazing like rubies.

Under a stool I could part of fronds
and watch the mariners
driven by undiscovered tides.
My Gran creaking with plates like an ironclad,
my mother billowing by in white.
I remember the last time.
There were sudden bells and shadows
and I was pitched out.
Hands plucked at me, faces soaked me,
I tried to swim but
like my father was drawn dizzily
towards the hard heart of the sun.

Saturday in the Western Bar

The Western Bar is the world pared
down to beer.
When you strip away the layers
of the afternoon like an onion,
the film of spray
arching from the wheels of buses,
the shoppers bubbling at doorways,
the smooth sound of Desmond Lynham
on a score of distant television sets,
there is always a bitter core
like this, who sit in the shadows
and the wallpaper spined
with nicotine,
flopping like dolls on their
tall stools, tumbling soft
as babies and spilling
along the long bar like beer,
or sitting, bit parts
in a never to be discovered film,
spitting words like glass
from bruised mouths and winking
at the Go-Go as, through gauzed
and ribboned light, the girl
on the slab turns
like meat.

A Present of a Submarine

The day I got it
I was in a lay-by,
a knuckle of tar near Lugar,
and the sun against the green slopes
of farms was yellow like butter.
I was on the back seat with the submarine,
black, with working parts, from the
poshest shop in Edinburgh, was on
my knees. I remember an open
window, blisters of heat on the dimpled
upholstery and sweat on my neck
and legs.
He said it was only a joke
and she said not the type of joke
I ever want to hear
and then there was no more wash
of cars or birdcalls but silence
like a choir in my head.

I fingered the long snout of
the submarine, the conning tower,
the propellers that moved,
the lines sleek as a fish.
That's it, it might as well be it
he said, and the door slammed,
and he strode into the grass like
a god decked in light
and when he swept his hand
in a final cutting motion down
I shook and let go of the cruel
prow at last
for the safety of tears.

Anglophobia

Sometimes, after ten pints of Pale in Mather's,
my pals and I discuss, with reasoned calm,
the origins of Anglophobia.

The philosophy was mother's milk to me.
Our cat was called Moggy the Bruce.
In 1966 my uncle Billy died on his knees
before the telly screaming 'It didnae
cross the line ye blind bastard!'
I remember my Grandad, seventy five
and ridged with nicotine, sitting, grimly watching
a schoolgirls' hockey match. Hands like shovels,
he'd never even seen a game with sticks,
but he was bawling 'Bully up, Fiji,
get intae these English!'

An expression of lost identity, they say.
Some identity.
We were the most manic crew of cut-throats
out, never happy unless we were fighting,
preferably each other; any venue,
Turkestan to Guadeloupe.
It was only after the Pax Britannica
that any of us had a free minute between rounds
to contribute to the culture of the world.

By some strange alchemy we had however found
the untapped source of arrogance and up
to our arses in mud we could thumb our noses
at the Florentines and all the other poofs
of the Renaissance and take some solace
from thumpings by our betters by claiming
moral victory; a piece of turf from Solway
Moss and the crossbar from Culloden.
But despite all that, and sober, the limp
red lions stir the blood and in a crowd of
fellow ba-heids I'll conjure up the pantheon
of Scotland's past and jewel it with lies.
Unswerving stubbornness.
I suppose that in the graveyard of nations
Scotland's epitaph will not be a volume
like the French but a single line:
'Ye'll be hearing from us.'

from *Tramontana*, 1990

Bad News about Suicide by Drowning

When the world was too much
I went to Palnackie.
I had a notion to die there in a rock pool,
my profile pointing exquisitely out to sea,
but when I lay down
I was harassed by a gang of gulls
honking in stereo
and butting the air with their skin heads.
When they'd gone,
to crap on a telephone box
or stick the beak in outside the chippie,
the sea shambled up
and spat on my shoes like a dosser,
mumbling, "Bohemia no got a coastline, then?"
This was dry humour from
an unexpected source.
It cracked the waves up,
and they thumbed their broken noses
from the bay.

On the Point

John Gordon is dreaming,
unfurled like a flag on Ardtornish Point.
His family came here
on holidays, parking their lozenge
of a caravan near needle cliffs,
in the lip of the gale,
only a toehold, a stone jammed
in the wheel, from disaster.
He dreams of his mother, legs laddered in light,
who barred the debtor's door
and swept up the summonses in the morning
in a small green tray,

of his father, who used oils thick as thumbs
and left a black trail
like a comet's: the sharp spines
of paint rearing like beasts,
the photographs in Palestine
astride that great horse,
Lawrence of Dumfries.
Whatever faults or virtues the pair of them
had owned John had forgotten,
if he ever knew,
and pared down to symbol, to private myth,
they stare like Errol and Mrs Flynn
from endless fields of Kodachrome.

John sniffs, as tiny boats hop
like sandflies in the slough of sea.
The more anchored he becomes,
the more he seems to see his wake,
the more he hears birds squealing
like chalk on the wall of sky
and sees the sun sweeping boys back for tea
when they didn't need to dream of summer.

In the Southern General

My mother's on the fifth floor.
She's calm, though there's a dull
fire in her eyes and her hair is slick,
spread like a crown on the pillow.
"The cats been missing you," I begin,
but she quickly interrupts,
"Grandmother came up last night.
She sat on my bed and played
the ukulele."
White as linen, I plump up
an encouraging smile.
"Mrs MacDonald's sent some chocolate."
"Yes, I'll see her when I get downstairs."

My mother believes her world
has telescoped to a single
block of flats and that everything
she's ever known is stacked
chronologically beneath her bed;
her mother washing clothes
in Alt Creich,
Mrs MacLeod reading to the class
in Gaelic from the Gospel
of St Mark and somewhere very close,
my sister snoozing in her pram
one sunny afternoon
in Morningside.

Her skin is darker;
thin and veined like leaves,
and she imagines herself suspended like
some delicate and drooping plant
high above her roots,
her life no longer a series of collisions,
of new beginnings, but a single line
you could trace with your thumb
or read like a sign outside the ward:
Down one flight for middle age,
access by lift to infancy.

In my shaken state
it's a convincing tale:
all the people and places that made her,
here to see how she turned out,
to play ukuleles on her bedspread
at the end.
There's only one mystery left;
upstairs.
I think it's the Nurses' Home
but I don't push the point: I have no desire
to know what grim things lie ahead.
"Go up and have a look," she says,
cheerfully, as I make to leave.
"And bring us back some lamb chops."

The Station Bar

It's not the real world,
that's for sure.
Here are the stateless leaving,
and not all on the railway –
some are on a journey quicker than that.

No-one sees them off.
There's no colour or crying,
only a last sour mouthful of sunlight,
a kiss of ash,
a *Daily Record* kicked around all week
and waving, limply.

Trains surround them
shuddering like dreams
but they no longer think of sailing
along the cold rails.
This is Terminus,
and through the plate glass
travellers hurry past the debris of the day.

Who Farted in Room XIX?

The Ufizzi, July 1988

Ghirlandajo's Madonna has gone quite green.
It can't have been the nuns;
zipped up tight in their white frocks
they are removed from this world by
high feats of tailoring.
Dresses stacked like sails,
they glide an inch above the ground
and their nostrils twitch in the airless room
with the aroma of another plane.

It wasn't St Sebastian.
His nose is turned up with the pure
stink of sanctity.
The Americans have turned from measuring
the stigmata to stare at me.
I shrug. Too much insalata my shoulders
seem to say but soon I am alone,
left in no doubt as to the place
of flatulence in devotional art.

Nevertheless the fruity smell
has raised some points.
For with all that greasy food surely the
saints themselves must have been prey to
the occasional blast, in which case is
it not a holy act?
Probably the Council of Niceae ruled that
the Apostles did not break wind. Poor sods.
But then this room with its squeaky
cartoon angels and it's dapper shepherds hasn't much
to tell us about the real world.
Dogma squeezes art flat.
I'm off to the Venetian Room, to see the
fat ladies. Give me pagan influences any time:
the smell of fart as well as flowers.

Marina

When I surfaced,
bloated with towels, eyes wrung out
and pressed between my palms,
Marina was singing somewhere,
a song about the sea.

Waterlogged,
I could see the lick of oceans
and Marina's cave
damp with tellin,
hung with little combs
made from cuttlefish.
I was dumb but I could feel her fingers
butting through a tangle of hair,
see her breast move in coral.

Years went by.
Continents were drowned,
Stars arced and sizzled out.
I said at last
"My ardour for you is such
that I will leave the shallow
world of men."
"Oh, that's nice dear"
she said, replacing the hairdryer,
"Do you want anything on it?"

Tommy

He came to school each morning in a hearse
(The firm did undertaking and taxi cabs were scarce)
and every time sank deeper
in dirty coils of anorak
so it sometimes seemed that from the dark
you could only see his eyes smoking
behind the tinted glass and folded wings
of leather.

At first, when there was still a gleam,
he drove through the estate
like a sheik burnoosed in his limousine,
straffing the houses and the wastes
with those eyes
but as time passed he realised
the funeral was his.

Tommy wore his scars with dignity,
defended his family,
his mum and dads,
liked animals,
loved history
and had an IQ of 153.

One exam time in May,
with the school shaking each sunny day
like a mirage,
Tommy had his chance of a new life, his ticket
out, and told us where to stick it.
Inside he was already dead,
and drew spiders on the page instead.

Salty

My history teacher was an old sailor.
At school assemblies, numb with praying,
I would look up and see him
straight and sharp as a tusk,
a glower scrimshawed on his face.

No singing:
he didn't believe in God.
He balanced on the lip of the stage,
legs astride as if to catch the swell,
and scowled down his pirate's nose,
defying them to produce the source
of all this whinging,

something as roaring as the sea,
or that Scandinavian wind
that howled through his teeth,
through the eyes licked by white hair,
and shivered our timbers.

His colleagues hated him.
They hinted at a weakness for boys,
whispered he was found at the end
in an indecent posture
(by some trick of pathology
clutching himself).

He was replaced by a man who ate Vick
and on a sepulchral Monday morning
God reclaimed his sea of bobbing heads
but I was at Salty's funeral
where thunder chuckled in the sky
and I saw the minister blanch,
drowned by a growl from the grave:
'Tell that bastard to stop talking
through his holy arse –
I died with a tiller
in *my* hand.'

An American Dream

Reading Bukowski,
drinking Michelob
and watching the sky
bounce away to the wide lapels
of the world
I was moved by a vision of America,
a pandemonium of blue and prairie gold
snapping past my eyes like film,
and I sniffed a freedom
born of space, or it's illusion,
then the guard announced "Kilmarnock,"
a sound like softly closing doors,
and when an old man asked
Is this us then? I had to say yes it was.

Natural Wastage

Mid July, and the streets are dry
as dust
though in the wash of traffic,
the white shell of brick and glass
and the pavement that bubbles
in the distance like melting
butter, there is a hint
of water, a promise that the drought
will soon end.

In the same hope
the hunters are here,
in doorways,
on their backs in the scrub,
whistling through the belly
of the day. They're here
on the advice of their organs,
those blunt and rubber totems
long on instinct,
short on sensibilities.

In this paralysis of heat
the girls are leaving school
for good,
teetering on their long legs,
pausing to sniff the stale
and thrilling scent of predators
before they dart into the dazzle
of the crowd, the many limbs
like long grass waving,
and, long before any frontiers
are reached, the teeth.

Majorettes

There's a ragged science.
Batons flirt with gravity
and bounce beyond the probability of hands.
Teeth shuffle into line
and wink like semaphore.
Slow as sleepwalkers,
the Lochside Leopards are probing
for rhythm in an overdose of base
while their brothers juggle with crisps,
leaving little mountains
for their mothers, erupting in applause,
to dust with ash.

The day isn't short of drama.
The janitor's had his eye put out
and there's a rumour that
one of the Teeny Texans is Rumanian.
Her beard seems a clear
infringement of the rules.
The committee will confer.

There is one girl
whose well-schooled teeth are hidden
in a frown of concentration.
She catches and throws
and follows the flight of the wand
as it spins in the cobwebs
and the fractured light
and returns perfectly to her palm.
She stalks off in silence.
The Dumfries Marching Band Association rules
may be vague on transsexuals
but they are explicit on those
whose horizons aren't low enough.

Love Poem

My love has gone.
Stars in the puddles guide her home,
the stinging rain on cobble stones.
Out of my sight she doesn't walk
but flies. Zodiacs bend in her wake.
She's pinned the moon on her shirt top
and trails her sooty feet on chimney pots,
and where she's brushed,
the night is black as diamond dust.

My love has gone
in a blaze of cider, with ash and cheery
embers of song and life in a beery
blast of noise curling after her like smoke,
like fingers tugging at her coat,
till a taxi hijacks her,
bears her back along the straight and narrow
where street lamps glower
and the wind's too genteel to tap on doors.

My love is gone but I can see her;
time is asleep in the sweep of an arm
and the town shuffles back, blinking in the calm,
tired as a pensioner.

Lindsay and Susan at Tyne Cot

Two up to the minute girls,
spikey hair and ra-ra skirts,
bopped through Belgium to Haysi Fantayzee
and found themselves
at the end of a tourists' day
at Tyne Cot.

They'd struggled off the bus
where many didn't – all miles merge in time,
all stops seem the same –
and as the wind rose
wandered through the graves,
small dark shadows
in a greater galaxy of white.

They fell quiet, and drifted.
Lindsay among the pale rolls of honour,
Susan before one simple stone:
A Soldier of the Great War.
Known unto God.

No name.
No face.
No hint of human story but
this boy reached out
and for a moment told of misery and mud
so sad a tale that Susan cried.

And as the bus revved
and friends hung out the windows
baying for their tea
the girls stayed long enough to write
Lindsay and Susan 1983
words cannot tell.

The Caulside Cafe

Under the plastic vines
and oilscapes, fat as your thumbs,
of the planet Mars,
men are watching the sun as it proceeds
calmly to the rhyme of bells
past the tidemark of another mewing Saturday,
the empty cans, the puddles,
and the windbags.

Some are still drunk.
They are anaesthetised
but can't bear the incision of the day,
others stare at their saucers
and long for the duff rationality
of beer.

Andrew and I eat our roll,
build our bricks,
and look at a bright swathe
of Sunday in Dumfries,
a puzzle not quite in place.

The Medium and the Mixture

Hole in the Wa' September 1986

This is not the Place Pigalle
but there are paintings here
in the curl of smoke, in the tints
and halo of light,
in the texture, thick as oils,
stale as cigarettes, old as wrinkles.
Three hundred years of drool have
made this place what it is. And
droolers; for this is a return
to childhood, to mouths, sucking
on glasses, ranting and smooching
like madmen muted by the world but
free in a raw sea of words till
darkness pulls the shutters down
and the last spilled sounds are wiped up
like drink from the bar,
and they shuffle out, soft as a
mumble, empty as babies,
every colour of the rainbow
but always brown as beer.

Some doomed civilisation lives here
and they behave as if each drink, each
belly laugh, is their last, wrung by sorcery
from the suffocation of days.
Old men with skin like vellum grab
your arm, catch your eye,
as if they believe they will not die
if they are talking.
There are some not so much washed up
as out of step; eccentrics to a narrow
fringe of saintliness, dreaming
aloud with words and fooling no-one.
Enjoyin yarsel? drawls Canada in his
star spangled shirt, tales rich as maple,
plenny of action dawntown.

Max is elbowing life into the accordion
and Canada jerks down the bar,
his hat cocked like Fred Astaire's,
his cuffs wet with whisky,
mouthing some Quebecois river song
he's learned on some sore and sober
morning at the library.
In the hard light from the dartboard
his face is full and yellow
like a doll's.
There's no wine bar neutrality here.
We're one step from the charnel
house, or one step from grace.
We know the score.

Echoes

In the television room with 5S.
Brown panelled walls, crisp packets
stuffed in the cracks like garlands
and narrow fingers of sun.

There's nothing to stir their emotions
in these images flickering across the screen,
the crushed skulls, the mud, the cratered fields
of crosses, safe in sepia.
There is a cosmic gap between these young
folk and mine, not expressed
in a mere seventy years of time.
They are history, these characters in
Charlie Chaplin brown, comically removed
from the Technicolor world,
and they are television, where suffering
is daily pared to something else.

The programme ends. Frowns give way
to talk of Morten Harket and
cocktail hour at Valentino's.
Yet Jill and Stewart and the rest
are not insensitive. They just can't
see beyond the fun, beyond the sun
of this Spring day, and here, at last,
with these ghosts on film, is common ground.

Making for Arcadia

Greece was on my mind yesterday:
the stabbing blues, the bustle
like a sea to drown in.
I caught the Piccadilly Line to Heathrow
and the hiss of closing doors
was like the wind in the cypresses
and my head bent dreamily to the warm
water prospects of the world
as if to a kiss.

As Hounslow I woke up
and the sky had darkened to a sweeping
crown of black. Rain pawed at the glass.
All the square jawed backpackers
had gone, spirited away, and, framed
in yellow light, the travellers were
a shabby frightful crew, huge bellied,
toothless, careering together like
the damned as the train juddered
screaming through a nightmare
of clouds, and leaves like hands
slid away from windows.

At the back, dressed in baggy trousers,
a bearded man gripped one of the spars like
a rudder. Light broke beneath his
steering arm and his cheerless
skirling laughter echoed through
the carriage as if through
endless hollow vaults.
Typical of Lunn Poly
not to tell me there was a stopover
for the over 30s.

Ten Past Eleven

Dickie's Bar.
Faces round as hops.
It is just after Eleven
and they are staring shyly at their drinks,
as if they had just been introduced,
or can't bear to remember last night's
passionate affair.

Outside, roads twitch by
like nerves,
cars nag, kids scream,
clouds fold over the sun
then unfold, like impatient arms.

Silence, for they are savouring
time with each thick mouthful,
drinking minutes.
Each belly talks of hours and days,
brags like a sailor about time
marooned from the world
in this land
where only the clock reminds,
tapping like a knuckle on the glass.

May Revision

Answers. Remember there are three,
one each from Sections A and B,
and one from those or Section C,
though that one could be
hard I reckon.
May revision,
the long days beckon.

Write lucidly, remember.
Fill the page.
be sure to know where
dates apply. Gauge
the time. You know the drill,
and can see the sun
spark clouds of broom on dreaming hills.

Remember Sarajevo. Who can say
the province that it sat in,
the time of murder, month and day,
and the name of the assassin?
Alison, you know better than to chatter
and stray to thoughts of love,
or sex, and things that really matter.

Hard work, remember.
That's the way you all succeed.
Don't you dare relax,
or heed
friends that do. And class,
don't dance on old chalk paths
or run stark naked through the grass.

Remember this, one last good luck.
Take two pens
and if you're stuck
move on. And if you've sense
move on, forget the lot.
Do your May revision
in an older school of thought.

Supervising S3 Science

I'm high above Dumfries
on a bleached spur of high technology
while the town leans
in a haze of chimneys and towers
like minarets and collapses, at last,
in a ruin of Aegean blue.

I sit in my old sandals
weaving threadbare nets from words
out of habit – few fish find their way
into these traps anymore –
while the girls wade ashore
through the heat like Gods,
skirts tied round their strong thighs,
their faces tanned and hard with light.
They have reduced the world
with their terrible eyes,
melted frontiers,
and they hold truth cooling
in their palms like ore.

Sarah breezes through the books,
the scripts scattered like totems
round my desk.
She's carrying a wire pot
she's plucked from the ceiling.
I am still trying to understand
how a light bulb works and Sarah
is swinging at arm's length, with
a matey carelessness, the structure
of the physical universe, the key to life itself.
It doesn't look too much;
a mesh of plastic balls.
I wouldn't have thought it could
hold a lobster, never mind
a generation.

1990

En route to culture,
I am derailed in Kilmarnock.
The buffet is like some recipe for Scotland:
two Labradors crossed in a reservoir of grease,
a drunk man swallowed by his toorie,
two infants dribbling on a sea of broth,
seventeen pints of lager,
the tang of tar and sweat and beans.

The minutes shuffle by
and hours kick like fractious children
at their skirts.
The room has a strange and stygian appeal,
a kind of alternative panorama
for shortbread tins.
"Aye, there's strong beer in all of us"
an old boy says.

I have to agree.
It's ten o clock.
On the boulevards the pie shops
are opening
and wet leaves are brushing through crowds
to all the gutters of Glasgow.

The End of the Road

How can the road end?
There's no more tar, that's all.
This last town in Scotland is no terminus,
the road runs gently into the sea
as if it was the most natural thing
to drive on to Norway, or to Labrador.

Over Lerwick, bent like an ear on the coast,
the gulls hang, their bone heads
set against gravity,
willing fat boats home down
the throat of the day.
Like the doors,
the people have no locks.
They are raw, but distance
has not rendered them quaint.
The morning news – *Clothes line near Tingwall*
Catches fire, a child's best jumper is burned –
doesn't make me laugh but rage
at all the other headlines in the world.

Oh what a breath of fresh air
is in these draughts from the north.
This is how we might all have been,
if we could have turned our backs,
if our nerves hadn't developed
faster than our heads,
if our eyes had been open to the sea
that beats like a heart here
even beneath the skin of the land.

from *Horridge*, 1994

The World Book of the McMillans

Dear **Hugh McMillan**,
you have been selected by our clan computer
to receive a copy of
The World Book of the McMillan's $149.95
(including unique hand painted coat of arms).
Have you ever considered, **Hugh McMillan**,
your family ties and heritage?
In these pages, **Hugh**,
you will bear witness to the heroism
and industriousness of your ancestors
and learn about the forebears
who shaped the history of the world,
like **Fergus McMillan, the 8th man of Moidart**,
Hector 'Steamboats' McMillan,
the inventor of the 12 Bore Scrotal Pump Beam,
Brian 'Big Shuggie' McMillan, Golf Caddie to the stars,
and many many others,
though probably not **Archie McMillan**
who died of silicosis
or **James and Colin** who drowned in the Minch,
or **Struan** who drank himself to death
in that corner of the Central Bar.
To bear witness to that kind of thing,
Hugh McMillan,
it costs a bit more.

Tam Rejects the Consolation of the Church

Okay, Christ suffered,
but only for three days,
and he didn't have to.
I know God gave his son for us
but it was the kind of death
a properly motivated man
might manage for a cause.

What kind of following would he have had
if God had reserved for his son
the kind of death that ordinary folk have to suffer,
some lingering terminal disease
where you can just drag yourself around
and no more, your guts and soul rotted away.

He had a crisis of faith
after a few hours.
My mother was eaten away for 360 days,
and not alone;
the rest of us bled to a kind of death
that made dangling on a piece of wood
look a dawdle.

I don't think he died for us:
I know he didn't die like us.

Old Bobby Spoils a Night Out

'You've got to give it to them,
though you hate the bastards.'
We are talking about Glasgow Rangers,
when Bobby, an old man
whose face has imploded round a Monty moustache
and a mouth liberated from teeth,
sits between us.
He is shouting
but not in a language that need words,
though I believe it is about the war,
and he is wearing the Africa Star.

We ignore him,
'They were lucky in the first half though...'
but Bobby is up, shadow wrestling.
He has these plastic slip-on shoes
and a sockless white ankle
protruding like a bone.
He's prodding it at our feet,
getting leverage,
tugging at something with his arms,
poking it, twisting it,
his mouth filling with spit.

'They did well, you have to say it.'
You have to say it
or see that brown blood in the sun
or his hand about to turn your face to his.
'What the fuck does he want? Absolution?
another medal?'
It's in his eyes what he wants,
it's in his eyes
like ice.
They did well the boys,
you have to say,
you have to.

Soor Faced Sue

Sue was at her worst with men.
When a new boy came onto the ward
you would get him to say hello to Sue
then stand back and watch the fun.
Hello, she'd murmur, then smile,
and lunge with blunt fingers at his eyes.
The Ashludie Kiss we'd call it.

She was a mad one,
but when she cried for her Ma
in the middle of the night
you'd swear it was a wee girl
and sometimes, like when
she had that minister by the chukkies,
shouting you fucking smarmy wee bald bastard,
she seemed the height of reason.

A Very Straight Line

In the parlour of the pub
the squirrel looped the same loop,
the morse of its belly
spelling out a monotonous distress,
front paws flip,
back paws down,
then blink,
at the same vista,
the blurred threat of a falcon
stuffed and primed,
the tatty drapes,
the light through brown bottled glass.

One day,
and I swear it was to spring me, not him,
I unhooked the cage.
He paused,
spun backwards,
and sped out the door
in one straight line,
and when he should have sensed the wheels
he didn't swerve
as if this trajectory
was what he'd dreamed of,
all our circular days.

The Black Gulls

Dumfries, the Old Bridge,
a thumbnail past seven,
the sun squeezing past confident clouds.
Lean over and see hidden trees
on the surface
moving without wind
and walls swimming
and gulls racing their blunt images
across the silence,
through the towers of the town
dreamily shaking,
and there, my head,
set square in the hieroglyph
of reed and water, in place.
How long passes?
There are homes and pubs
and people waiting
but the black gulls, their flight is perfect,
matching dip and dart and distance,
and never leaving
the rapture of the dark.

Sundown

It is nearly night,
the sun is calling home the light
through minarets of metal and wire,
through hills quietly sleeping,
through street lamps blinking
in the dips of distance,
through regiments of trees
dragging their heels
and seagulls nagging
at the scorched hems of fields.

Opposite, in the melt
of the train's neon
and a last sunlight
pale as a pearl above the beard of cloud,
another beloved landscape.
Hair like embers, head unbowed,
who will call you to sleep?
Only I will see that miracle;
the darkening of that star.

Play

We sit, my son and I,
on the train from Larbert,
playing with our toys.
He has Bret the Hit Man Hart
and I have a new can of export,
bright as a pillar box.
Haaaa he whispers, haaaaaaaa.
It is the noise of a crowd in his head.
It has a large capacity his head,
all seated like Ibrox Park.
I myself am waiting for the plastic tag
that bears the letter X.
It is on the bottom of the can
and will win us a holiday in Barbados
at the liver unit of my choice.
While we play, Scotland flicks unnoticed by,
its fins of frost, trees cupping cold hands,
living rooms stiff with Sunday,
then we bounce into Glasgow.
"Still time" he says, "still time"
and Bret lunges for a Clothes Line
or is it a Folding Body Press? I don't know,
I am watching foam recede from
a smooth and endless shore.
No X, only a blurred reflection
of a place, a person, I should be.

Surprise Attacks

I hear the sound of a boy
waiting to be ambushed
by his father,
that carpet of smells and roars
like a bear, all hugs and stubble.
Each step breaks on the stairs like ice
and it precedes him, this excitement,
like a shadow mad and off its moorings.
Oh should we not weep
for the ghosts of undiluted joy
and the years I cannot wish for him
but he is eager, all fists, for.

It is a long minute.
He is stopped, poised on one leg
like a crane.
Perhaps he will be a dancer
or a poet
it doesn't matter.
Whether he requires it for his art or not
he will be ambushed by his father,
from the tips of pencils
the precipitation of sleep
he will be ambushed by his father,
when he is old and threadbare
and sick of such surprises,
even then
he will be ambushed by his father.

The Fire and the Flowers

We slow down
and the sun bounds down the train.
In a field below the embankment,
an angle of light and flowers,
there are two boys.
one is lining up a penalty,
the other, a year or so smaller,
is swaying, ready for the save.
Overhead the clouds are high,
fragmented, like string.

We inch past
as the boy runs up.
A breeze sets the white flowers off
like applause.
I add larch to the scene
in a long fringe to the left,
some houses behind.
I press my face against the glass
and see the kick,
head-high to the goalie's right,
a great shot.
I see him leap, his hand curve,
I see it and the ball blaze
in the white of the sun.

Then they're gone.
There's no save, no goal,
only the beat of the train
and the countdown to Kilmarnock,
only deadly logic to suggest
an end to such dynamics.

The Window

Opens upwards,
scorns gardens cowed by fuchsia,
hosepipes, cars parked too perfectly,
the cramped sounds and sizzles,
of tea-time in Dumfries,
the bleeps, the woofs, the tinny tunes,
the children crying.

It is an invitation for clouds
to peek like school kids and run away,
for sudden sunlight and a rhythm line of rain,
for breeze to gently take the piss

and sometimes at night
it opens up
as if all the stars had to look at was us,
and only the gossip of leaves
reminds us there are other points of view.

In the Frame

Staring at that slice of blue cloud
and the sun hung like an onion
between half-lengths of lamppost
and the strange stalks of buildings.

There is a maniac muttering in my ear,
the way maniacs in toilets do,
some homily about piss
or hurrying back for beer.

But it is better here,
where you can't see the doorsteps
that daily clamp this sandwich in place,
where for a moment you can escape the frame

and there seem such possibilities
for you and I
in the arrangements of clouds and sky
and the distant base of engines

from a road I could draw just there
in that gap between the window and the Xpelair,
draw it between the hems of stone and briar,
like a crowbar.

A Wee Word

Dear Sir, a member of the School Board –
who must remain faceless –
saw you cuddling Miss Dewar
outside the Dumfries Arms last night.
He was passing in a fast car
and wasn't really looking
but saw you stroking her hair
and nuzzling that little diamond of neck
with your nose,
and you a married man.

Given such examples
our pupils may no longer be content
to conjugate, to add or subtract,
to think modestly in French.
They might conclude that loving
dark haired girls in public is a good idea;
that it's possible for a grown man
to be weak, or wrong, or dreaming still.

Where would all this end?
It would no longer be safe to walk
the streets after badminton.
We would no longer be secure
in our bungalows,
worse,
in our pronouncements.

Readings of October

Once more, October,
with its squalls
and secretive moon.
I'm staring at these walls,
the orange flowers, the damp,
the dunts, the dud starts.
How could anyone sit in this room
and not see it unroll from right to left,
a personal makimono?
Because it is dead,
beyond decoding.
Upstairs, asleep, a new literature
is born from these scraps
but on my horizon
there is only a red balloon,
lashed to a clothes line
furiously signalling,
dipping at the mud
then straining for a glimpse
up the cuffs of cloud.

Turning Taps

It is Tuesday, cold,
the last clouds are cardboard,
the moon a carved hole in ice.
I walk down this street with its red brick,
its certainties sandwiched in sandstone
and it's hard to think of denouements,
but for once it's clear;
there is ritualism,
I have to turn the taps.

We sit, drink tea.
Dumfries kneels down to darkness
and it's difficult to see your face,
its sad beauty.
Things unsaid, said too often,
turn in the air like glass.
I've been with you too long,
too little, you say,
though it's the same.

Pinch faced I go to drain the taps,
and free another house
of magic.

Letter from the 24th Congress of the Communist Party

Dear Joe,
Sorry you couldn't be here,
you really missed yourself.
Krupskaya brought a quiche
but the fun really started when Bukharin
told the joke about the dyslexic deviant functionalist
and when Dzerhinsky got his cock out,
turned his pockets inside out
and pretended to be Babar,
I thought I'd die.
Who said the inevitable victory of the proletariat
was bound to be joyless?
Love Vlad

Dr Gallagher, I Presume

He is crumpled in tropical fawn;
dressed for a safari.
He sits in Ruby's
besieged in a kraal of black-ribbed chairs
by winking bandits,
blow-piped music,
the long and lustrous thighs of girls.

They are trying to blast his head off with heavy metal
but he will not shift.
As an anthropologist, he has danced to beats.
'John Lennon' he muses,
'that takes me back a few wives.'

Like a river, life buffets the door.
We hear parakeets screaming
from distant bungalows
and the drum of rain on cobblestone.
'*Une autre fois?*' he asks,
and when he taps the glass
it gleams like diamond in the dark.

Tour 4150

A metallic voice in the heat
and heavy throb of engines:
'Behind that wood is Belsen,
the German camp.'

The courier waves sleepily
and a few necks crane,
cameras twitch and are still.
They halt by wet trees,
by miles of black ploughed earth.

'Good to stretch your legs' they say,
and patrol the side of the road,
anxious for the bus to open again
like a womb.

A few rattle the branches,
wrinkle their noses,
but what they smell is burnt toast
in the Rasthaus,
not history.

Rejoice, there is a Jugglers' Shop

Rejoice,
there is a jugglers' shop
that sells padded balls and flasks,
kites and yo-yos.
Before I saw it,
horrors were in my head,
Tuzla, Nova Bila,
battles for dignity and life itself,
but we can relax,
there is a jugglers' shop
where the concerned can gather
to discuss juggling,
the cost of nocks and ferrules,
the effects of the SB-2,
the yo-yo NASA recommends.
Don't you know that the yo-yo
represents the spinning miracle of life,
it connects us with that inner space
within us all which is always
spinning and dancing.
No?
Then rejoice,
there is a jugglers' shop.

Ideal Homes

You keep the Subaru,
compact as yourself,
white as the knuckles on the wheel,
shouting north over the Corinth Canal,
over the bleached bones of Greece,
through mountains alight.
I look into your eyes,
beyond the reflection of that farm truck
with brake problems.

Three days ago, in the Cyclades,
a huge sun sank on cue
and a breeze carrying all the hot bubble
of the Peloponnese fanned my cheek
and I thought yes, yes, this is the place
but now I look into your eyes
I see a darker climate,
and I am more disposed to live there,
with all its squalls.

The Moon over Constanza

The moon over Constanza
looks like a hole drilled in space by a genius
but Captain Fluoriu is earthbound
and as water – or oil – or aviation fuel –
drips from the roof of the Boeing onto my salami
and the man who looks like Francis Coppola
weeps gently into his half-filled beaker of wine
I keep my eyes pinned on the moon above Constanza,
even after it is sliced in two by a wingtip
and on our backs,
even after the plane has slewed to a halt
beside a walnut tree and a dog
searching in a universe of fleas,
even after that.

Death on the Nith

The fans on the ceiling blur silently,
lift the hair of the brown-eyed girl
in the floral skirt drinking tea.
Through the fretwork of chair,
long legs earth on white tile.
Outside, in a blaze of sky,
two chimneys pretend to be pagodas.
Don't these children arguing the toss
chirrup like cicadas?
And isn't the breeze outside
playing through manicured gardens,
rattling through the acacia,
like a clock running slow?
No.
The man at the counter
buying a doughnut and hot Vimto
has no parallel in the east.
Soon he will read his *Standard*
and cough into that brown hankie
he's tugging from his coat.
He will bring the rain,
the muggy wind from the Solway,
the tinny chimes of the Midsteeple
playing Bonnie Gallowa.
He will eat his pastry next to me
and think the blood on his hands
is jam.

A Cultural Exchange in Scotland

I am walking down Irish Street,
the road that's only wide enough
for three of four lorries and a pipe band,
when I am jostled by a drunk.
He looks at my shoulder bag
of soft Cordoba leather.
'What are ye?' he asks, 'a poof?'
Fuck off!'

'Sir' I respond.
'Only a week ago I sat
in the Patio de Los Naranjos
as water turned to light in Al-Andalus
and the word of 'Abd Allah ibn 'Amr
shone like quicksilver in my head.

Three days since,
in the ruined gardens of Medina Azahara,
I saw the desert stretch like serenity
while cicadas sang.

Just yesterday in La Alhambra,
the sky unrolled at my feet
round myrtle and jasmine
and the tip of heaven seemed only
a finger's span away...

and you're telling me to fuck off?
You fuck off!'

Pictures in the Fleshers' Arms

On a bench ringed by a picket fence
the Provost sits
beneath a telescopic hat,
his legs, like a sea-captain's,
comfortably astride,
a deed or writ clutched to a well-stuffed chest.
His collie dog,
head on the Provost's knee,
looks back at the camera
with the sharp white of its eyes,
it's devotion only comprehensible
when you see, on close examination,
the Provost standing on its cock.
On the right,
A man with a bonnet is limping off frame,
slowly, as you would expect
if he had great respect for the Provost,
or a long flat cock
and legal notice to quit stuffed nearby.

Also in the frame,
on top and looking used to it,
is his wife.
She is dressed sombrely,
her wide skirts merging with shadow,
the table in the foreground
metamorphosed to gloom.
There is a white hat with flaps
that reach her waist

though it seems clear she owns no anatomy,
her body having become, through constant virtue,
metaphor.
Her brows are cosh thick,
her eyes banked, deposited.
In her right hand she holds
a thick and heavily bound book,
no prizes for guessing.

And there is a child in pantaloons.
He is being held tightly by a muscled woman,
one hand around his waist.
She is the product of some scheme
to mix the genes of Calvinists
with those of German discus throwers
to create the perfect nanny.
The boy is suspended over the grass,
and he is staring down at the manicured lawn,
sensing the attraction of freefall
but knowing they will never let him go.

Marking

I go along the Whitesands
every night when all the kids
have gone to bed
and with a pencil torch
and heavy duty marker-pen
ease my way past cobblestones
and empty cans of coke
to scan the walls for this,

here, some new work,
blistered black across the plaster,
TEACHERS ARE CRAP.
I smile.
YES INDEED THEY ARE
I write below,
TEN OUT OF TEN,
YOURE REALLY LEARNING NOW.

Hammy and the Dog

There's an old man in the corner
with thick glasses
and a parka flecked with mud,
sitting, laurel led in smoke.
He's mouthing to a collie across the way
and though there are no words,
you know he's telling it things
about his life in Locharbriggs,
giving warnings about owners, bitches.
The dog, trapped between the legs of a yapper,
stares past the fire into Hammy's smoky eyes,
glad, for once, to be having
the loudest conversation in the room.

Mon Cher

The poet's final letter exists only in the shape of
a fragment addressed to his friend Stuart 'Shug'
Hanlan. It is invaluable in helping to understand
the state of mind in which he undertook his final
fateful journey by steamer to the Stewartry.

... Mon Cher,
my senses deranged by a cold sore,
I have left the bourgeois life of Dumfries,
with its stockbroker cottages and men with balaclavas
to live a dissipated life
among the highly coloured shacks
and bayous of Wigtownshire.
My brother wanted me to train with Fastfoods
but I said no, I will write,
writing is my life,
I must follow the lyrical movements of my soul,
and so I am here, among the gulls.
I have taken as a mistress a half-caste bar girl,
Jean MacDougall, she is my muse.
I write, ah how I write,
my fingers ache,
but already my opus, 'The Flowers of the Machars',
has been accepted by Ladybird...

(Here the manuscript ends)

from *Aphrodite's Anorak*, 1996

Leaving Scotland by Train

It's not easy.
Near Perth there's a conspiracy
of gravity and guilt
that propels me forward in my seat
to squint at my motherland
from a foetal position,
my nose snorkelling through the coffee
and the world whirling backwards,
disappearing gaily down some Scottish plug hole,
an Omphalos near Denny
where the land is conjured back
with all the sheep and the seagulls and the trees
still buttoned on it,
and broken down to formless green.

I daren't open my eyes
in case it's really done the trick
and I'm bobbing like a peeled lychee
in the gynaecological soup,
a heart pulsing in my ear
and a gentle voice saying:
'Where do you think you're going, you bastard?
Stay here. Where it's warm.'

Willie

'Drunk or sober,
yon man could pit a carpet boul
or a keystone richt oan the button.'
Willie is nodding modestly
in the Fleshers' Arms,
70 proof, if he's a day.

Willie doesn't age.
Like his dykes, he weathers.
He hasn't lost his hair,
but mislaid it in an absent minded way:
it's strung up there somewhere
on the rich topography of scalp
as thick as ever, but vitrified,
as impenetrable as his handiwork.

Below it, creases run
through the skin
like dry river beds.
There are hard callouses
round the smile
that defines and defies his history.

His face is a map
and like all landscapes
is variable.
Willie hasn't always been good.
I think he predates such concepts.
He is both sides of a very old coin.
The man *is* Galloway.

Dundee Jute Mill, Turn of the Century

They stand crucified by loom ribs and spindles,
these hemp women made from shadow,
with their skull heads doubled over machines
that worked, but not for them.
They present their misery unabashed,
unwilling to hide it,
unable to conjure, for a shutter second, smiles.

In the foreground there is a youth.
He is small
(The nearest women are bending to his height)
but there is more than a hint of swagger
in the watch chain,
the slightly bending knee,
the hand laid proprietorially on a spool of cloth.
He is a golden boy:
he shines even in this glory of sepia.

It is the way the world is:
and you know the women will die
near the looms,
their certainties the more enduring,
and that the boy's chest will be torn
by machine guns,
all the puff and pride blown to smoke forever.
He will not live to see the skeleton of his mill
or hear the women, weeping still.

Monday Midnight

Through the window
the houses shift; a dreamy selentropy.
Stairs hung with creepers vanish
in starlight and smudge.
The night is heavy,
the birds and I squeal beneath it.

Just then I imagined you were laughing
and, for once, it was like knives.

In a little puddle of light,
surrounded by the boxes
you brought ashore like from a shipwreck,
still unpacked,
I sit and I dream
of syssarcosis.

Saturday 21 May

Leaving Dundee;
crows dummy run at fence posts,
the fields stretching flat as you can imagine
to the shapes of hills.
Little chimneys peep out, coy in trees,
and horses bend their heads.
Opposite, sombre suited,
some apparatchiks discuss the death of John Smith.
The emotion in Scotland, they say,
it is the mark of the man.
Perhaps, though it is more than that, and less.
Today, in the graveyard of the kings,
they are burying the perfect head of state for us,
unburdened by the inconvenience of public office,
a leader who never was,
of a country that is,
and isn't.

The X Files: Bonnybridge, October '95

Lorrayne
before you hit me with that object
shaped like a toblerone
let me explain.
We only went for a half pint and a whisky
then set off home but somehow
lost two hours on a thirty minute journey.
My mind's a blank
but Brian clearly saw
aliens with black eyes and no lips
leading us onto a kind of craft.
I tried to lash out, explain that I was late,
but they used some kind of numbing ray on me:
it put me in this state.
Lorrayne, don't you see what it explains?
All the times I crawled home with odd abrasions.
Put that down Lorrayne,
don't you see I *have* to go again,
for the sake of future generations.

What you Feel like When you get Eaten by a Bear

July,
the moon high above rags of cloud.
I was swinging a bag,
some crushed rubbish ready for the skip,
and I was thinking,
even in these mountains with the smell
of burnt wood and flowers,
about Rangers, how much I hated them,
and whether, back at the bar,
they would think my drink was finished
and take it away,
when suddenly I saw a bear,
standing two, three feet above me,
mouth shining,
eyes rolling like marbles,
a Brown Bear, a Carpathian Bear,
the type that follows Romanians home
as a matter of course and eats them.
And in that calm when the nerves,
mugged by alcohol, are like ice,
there was a moment when I felt
I suppose like those boys at Toubacanti,
one moment embarking at Leith among
the gulls and smell of fish
the next dodging with naked Indians
between red legged mangroves

swiping at conquistadors,
there was a moment,
at the teeth of it,
when I felt
Scottish.

Hans from Wuppertal

Hans from Wuppertal they called him,
in the bare-bulb nights in camp,
Hans who tells stories.
Long into the evenings
with ice patterning on windows
he would spin them tales
of the forests of Thuringia,
dark tales for the dark.
Hans from Wuppertal, they would say,
Hans the liar.
After the war, in Brooke Street,
in his little room filled with stamps,
he would tell stories too,
about flying planes in the war,
planes with no propellers.
Oh Aye, we'd say, Hans the Liar.
After he died, his sister,
whose letters he had returned unopened,
told us he was the Reich's favourite Test Pilot,
aide de camp to Goering,
Hans, it turned out, from Wannsee.

Reflections on the Aphrodite of Rhodes

Thoughtful tourist,
musing on the transience of grandeur, pause.
Forget the swelling of my breast,
the thighs' white gloss,
the impish angle of my chin,
and look, as I hold it out, at my hair!
Knots of string,
and no wonder;
it's hard to keep a coiffeur intact
two thousand years below a tobacconist's.
I used to look quite good, in fact,
like that bitch Tiramanitis,
all curls and clasps and look at the smile.
Now I'm only fit for this glass case,
the wanton part of a before and after piece
on Hellenistic Style.

History at Knossos

History is the thing that translates cow pats
into frescoes of rent boys and bimbo snake goddesses.
It's the thing that turns quarries into colonnades
guarded by men in underpants from C and A's.
History is maladjusted Victorians
thinking their wives were Helen,
their mothers Pasiphak,
and their penises the source of centipedes and scorpions.
History is that Spanish guide with the parasol
stamping near the site of the first flushing toilet,
shouting *Aqui! Aqui!*
Here sat King Minos.

Targets

I have this picture,
set against the penetrating greens
that memory ignited;
my dog running towards me
six inches above the Birks of Aberfeldy,
the berk of Aberfeldy,
rotor ears and tail
and tongue like a red banner,
beating the air,
advancing frame by frame
his bullet head cocked
at the centre of the lens,
daring my attention to wander off line,
to forces more fatal than gravity.

Aine

There's a dazzling slick of light on the water
as if some unlagged pipe has burst
and the sun is bubbling out.
It's nearly November
but summer is hanging over Oban
like a comic ending the season on a private joke.
Trippers swelter on the esplanade
in tweeds and cable stitching,
shake their heads,
wonder if David Icke wasn't right about the weather –
and if the water round Kerrera – deepest turquoise –
isn't proof of it.
But if they looked above their papers at the right
moment,
if they'd drunk the right amount of Bruachladich,
if their grannies had once been snogged
by the wild west wind,
they might see the cause,
strolling in that crook of tar
between the Dog Rock and Dunollie,
miracles in her canvas bag
and fire, summoned through the wands of masts,
burning in her hair.

Address to a Galway Pen

A poem was on my neck like a bat,
but in the barnyard of William Street
it squirmed away.
Now, in the boozy light,
you glint, not nicely.

Oh don't leave me like the others,
in Ladbrokes, or a warm pub,
or in some cafe folded to the breast of a crossword,
don't get lost in my lining and burst,
or desert me for a postcard writer;
such work is not for you,
your sleek lines gleam with pub light,
stars ripple in your length,
there is magic in you.

You could carve me metaphors
that would get my work snapped up,
praised by eggheads,
printed in anthologies,
or listen, one night
with the moon swimming through glass,
perhaps at a table like this
beaten down by elbows,
haunted by beer,
you could write

and what you write
might pierce the heart of the paper
like a sharpened stick
and the need to break the skin
would bleed, at last, away.

Easdale

A jetty, and stumps of cottages
in the wind, doors
gaping like mouths.

On one window, a shred of curtain
is still stuck on the glass. Smudged blue,
like babies' eyes, it belies the museum
calm, speaks of children
nursed here, not imported half made
from Guildford.

Across the sound a coach spills
its tourists on the Arts
and Crafts. They are searching for
the spirit of the Highlands, long gone,
like the miners, like the tide,
quiet as ledgers.

Getting Too Late For Football

Clouds shoulder the moon
and the sky is bruising
scarlet no navy blue.
The town, tiny in the palm of hills,
thins to silhouette,
the broken fingers of the trees,
the spires, the stubs of houses,
all blending to an aromatic
chocolate brown
with me in the middle,
vanishing like the dot on a TV screen –
a diminution signifying
more this time than a memory of bedtime –
and it's only the nagging cold,
the dull gleam of the football
and Andy calling from the
elbow of a goalpost for one last kick
that remind me
there are still things to do
and a route to try and find
through the dark.

Blethers

For two nights
I've teetered on this page
high above bronchial trucks
and winking snugs.
I've doodled and dribbled
an incontinent love
and out of it came a poem,
a piece of literary machismo,
that was to leave you breathless.
My, you would gasp in awe,
that fairly sums it up.
What rot.

You have given me your heart.
I see it in your worried eyes,
in the slow detonation of your smile.
I see it even here
in the soot and stones,
through gangling miles of cloud and sea.
What's a poem compared with that?
Blethers.

On the Hoof

I'm leaving Stranraer, replete,
the ribs of my last meal rattling at my feet.
Outside the bus there are layers of light,
fields are salt white,
the sea is dark as caramel.
A few trees dip tall
heads like parasols high
in a cocktail of clouds and streaky sky.

The girl opposite, nibbling a roll,
has hair that gleams in little seams like coal
as she bends down.
Her eyes are warm, her skin toast brown,
and I am reminded that all in all
there is enough in the south west
for everyone to digest;
the poet and the cannibal.

Louisiana Train

Funnelling through the night,
suddenly the lights shut off.
I lost sight of my maps, my beer,
the old lady with the rings,
the black eyed girl sad I was so ugly,
and instead the nearest thing
was a horizon burning with orange
and a thumbnail line of hills
bending round the moon,
and it was suddenly like Falkirk,
Falkirk for fuck's sake,
coming to Falkirk on a Saturday in winter
with the results on the teleprinter
and you in that green euphemism of a car,
that excuse for a birl against the odds,
ticking in the car park like a bomb.
Then the lights came back,
too late,
and the train surged on into the body of the night
with me sticking in its throat.

History

The last whaler lives
in a cottage with black sills
sunk like a bad tooth on Henry Street.
The other houses gleam in a practiced smile
that brings tourists to one side,
and artists to a salon on the other.
The street no longer stinks of blood
but peppermint.

The whaler has a wicker chair
and a bottle of beer stashed below.
Fuck youse, he shouts at the trippers,
at the bohemians fleeing with their paints,
fuck youse all
and he grins the wet width of his gums.

In the craftshop
among the pictures of local characters
there are no entries
for the year our man was born,
on the beach, they say,
in the shape of a dog.
After all, is it the kind of thing
you want to hear on your holiday,
a pensioner urging you to abandon
the Museum of Automata
to go instead and fuck yourself?

They are waiting, waiting,
for an incident serious enough
to have him removed,
strangled in his bed by a hit-man
from the National Trust
and replaced, no fuss,
with a hologram or a polystyrene head
that says

Hello Boys and Girls
come in and see my life:
it was hard but we had fringe religions
and folk music,
peppermint and little crosses made from jet
some of which are on sale inside
for as little as three quid,
for history surely

a small price to pay.

At the Swings

Puddles,
and bracelets of scuffed bloom.
The wet trees butt water
and the river noses past the bridge,
the arches stubbled with moss,
to where reeds swim with sandstone
in a black mirage
and only the punctuation of swans,
bent like question marks,
dazzle.

He swings,
his bright red shoes a challenge
to the consensus of cloud and
the wash of grey and green.
He stretches out his hands,
palm outwards,
'I can let go, and hold onto nothing.'

He's kept me moored like a full stop
on this page
that he'll desert one day
without a thought.
There's colour in the world,
a dazzle of colour,
but where could I go to see
such a brush stroke,
bold against the sky?
I could let go,
but I would hold onto nothing.

Angles

Three window panes,
a triptych of smithereens,
of sun on water,
gulls tight-roping on mastheads,
hills groggy with sandstone
gawping at the sea,
and the Sound of Kerrera
careering away like a big laddie
to butt the Hebrides.

Nearer, through the third pane,
a muddle of shadow and light,
the room bounced through a riot of glass
onto a wall outside.
No tourists look in here,
only I can detect an infinity of you,
your smile blazing to pinprick size,
to tickle dimensions beyond the glamour
of eyeshot.

Shug, Alex, Jock, Willie...

Hang about my head like shoplifters.
I have to follow them,
escort them firmly from my mind.
If I relax they'll have my imagination up their jouks
in a jiffy and be running up the road.

Most of the time they're safe on Kodachrome,
prison striped with sunlight,
or caught rat-eyed in cellar bars
but sometimes in my dreams they visit me.
Draped in woolly blankets
they ask formal questions about the price of fish,
boast of slippery girls,
songs they've shared with whales.

They shake their arms at me
and wail about the folk who've pilfered their identities,
use their names to prop up bills
and business cards
and the little things they send you
when you're books are overdue.

What do you want, I ask of them.
You, they say.
You,
and our time again.

Lyn Wilson Says a Prayer for Robert Burns

In St. Michael's they are commemorating Burns.
The sun fires corkscrews of dust
as cameramen tussle
and the static screams.

A Minister directs the telescopic lens
to the pew where Jean and Robert sat.
The man himself is gone.
He will be reconstituted later, like a burger,
from scrapings on the studio floor,
but now…

Behind me,
in an old blend of wood
and light thrown through green windows,
a young girl sits in prayer.
Her head is bent. Her hair is like a flame.

Beauty,
and bedlam.

A commemoration after all.

The Little Summer of San Demetrios

In the little summer of San Demetrios
sun ignites shale,
waterfalls drop like dull fire,
embers toppling at the end of a blaze.
We climb through light
to the coolness of river pools.
Below, cars blow along the road like dust.

Hours pass.
In the little summer of San Demetrios
your lips are like fruit
and your eyes rapt,
following the curve of hills,
the road that sloughs to Moffat,
the way back.
Come on, I say, *let's go on,*
the little summer of San Demetrios is for travellers.

Night is coming,
wind doubles the grass.
It is the way; the eye is closing.
It is time for going home, you say,
the little summer of San Demetrios.
Clouds gather, slowly join.
There will be such darkness
and for the lost, rain.

The Cargo of the 'Hopeful Binning of Bo'ness', Bound for the Darien Peninsula, 1699

140 periwigs
26 camel coats
210 Broons Books (Large print edition)
3 Gross string vests (should have been 3 gross string vests?)
25,000 Jean Redpath CDs
184 bundles of kindling
406 tea towels
1 accordion
120 copies of 'Trainspotting' by Irvine Welsh
    (Dutch language version)
4 brillo pads
1 Lena Martell Old Rugged Karaoke Video
4,020 sets of dominoes
and
some loose change.

As We Go Home

Rain grazes the road,
cuts its way to the valley
where Dumfries is lighting up
like an old man,
in coughs and starts.
We pass a tree,
a bag spread-eagled in the branches,
a sign nailed to its chin,
Fear Ye the Lord.

Yesterday the trees were like sails
on the Ramblas
and the sun too was silk
and yes there were plastic bags
but not bayonetted like this one,
empty ribs swinging on a gibbet,
half the logo gone,
HAD...
Haddows,
Or Hades.

Fear Ye the Lord
and the clouds gathering
as we go home.

In Search of Leanne

Remember? She was the one
whispering in my ear on the West Coast Line,
delivering me, on the same plate,
visions of Winter and Spring?
She was the one that shook the flowers,
parted the clouds to show
the slow and splintering world.
Where is she?
I thought she lived for my visits,
spent the times in between growing mushrooms,
or lighting the dawn around Barrhead.
I hope she's not defected:
Her intercession would win Pete Fortune
the Scottish Book Award that I deserve,
and what would become of her?
He would use her endlessly.
Unlike me,
her chaste lover.
I used to brush her lips,
there, like that,
a very small kiss,
enough,
for a poem to come.

Hole in the Wa' – April '96

Four o'clock.
Outside, kids rush back from school
and arrowing geese scorn thermals
home in a blur of blue
but here in a light like an old Master's,
scuffed by years or boots,
they are standing,
elbows hooked like batwings on the bar,
Tucker,
George,
the Major,
Annie,
turning noses into beer,
beer into spit,
life into shadows,
a day into dreaming.

So George, scarlet faced,
paces the bar like a poop deck
while the Major sways in his wake
and Hammie screams like a mandril
and Willie Gail sings,
his finger in the sticky air
scratching time to whole forgotten words

and Tucker, bent legs bowed,
will tell you his day,
the crowd not ba' heids in newsreel brown
but folk glorious in maroon,
the sun full on their faces, cheering
as Tucker cuts, in brilliant green,
his piece of ancient history
and the man with the hat
shows snaps of his grandson
who is mostly seven
and sometimes called Steven
but who always calls him Poppa,
not the man with the plastic bag
whose forehead kisses the bar,
but Poppa.

And so it is,
and time never passes here,
no-one dies,
but is replaced

and time never passes here,
only clocks move dark hands
round and round,
like other people's lives.

Saturday Afternoon in the Grotto

Santa's in Sauchiehall Street.
There's a file of cheery white face boys
with convicts cuts and little oval heads like eggs
and bright red freckles,
as if someone had stood at the front of the queue
with a paintbrush, flicking it.

Their dads, more used to snug bars than grottos,
are wheezing and stamping with the cold,
playfully cuffing ears,
sharing in the seasonal enthusiasms for chimneys
by smoking like them.
The result is a surreal and Scottish kind
of Christmas ambience

with rubber reindeer lurching drunkenly
through the fog
and tattooed men crunching, blind, through
polyester snow, scything down the penguins
and eyeing up the elf who's taking photographs:
give her a ride in my sleigh anyday.

It's happy enough
but I am a father of a more modern calibre
so I was disappointed to see Andrew vault
like a paratrooper from Santa's knee,
pick a handgun from the box
and cock it jauntily at the girl behind the Polaroid
as if to say:
not much call for the Spyrographs this afternoon,
is there Doll?

Happy New Year

Dumfries: midday.
When I lift the blind the room gets darker.
Outside, little trees skinned to a T-Shirt of bark gather
like casuals, chatter in the wind.
In the background, caged Christmas trees glimmer.
This is Scotland, January 3rd.
It looks like a landscapes tricked by germ warfare,
stripped of warmth, colour,
any signs that in the rest of the world pass for life.
Midday, midnight:
In the distance two men in anoraks converge,
to strangle each other.

from *After the Storm*, 2005

Wandered

He is visiting his old mother.
Sunlight is fading, leaves crunch under his boots.
When he arrives she is standing by the window,
tapping her small foot.
'Where have you been this last twenty years?'
she asks, anger in her dark and skittish eyes.

It is an old scenario.
The truth will only breed confusion,
worse, a dreadful sadness.
'I have been in orbit', he replies,
'It is the longest manned flight in space
by any Scotsman'.

She squeezes his arm,
Her face soft as a girl's.
'I am proud of you Willie', she says,
'I never doubted you would return',
and they sit and watch
as the stars come out over Gorgie.

Passage

Alex had been shrinking,
his skin turned transparent,
as though you could see through him
to the buses, the rain pearled shop fronts.
No-one mentioned it, though,
and every morning he came down,
stood at the bar with his mates,
paid his round.

But his voice became a whisper,
and through his neck,
fine veined and fragile as a leaf,
you could see it,
thin as a wafer,
more certain than bullets.

His friends, rough as they come,
whispered with him,
murmured like monks,
a soft litany
in the beery noise,
and at last,

when he had only one story left,
of leading his father
blinded in the war,
through Leith streets lathered
with sun, they'd only nod, wave
big hands as if easing the way.

While Ian Dunbar sleeps

While Ian Dunbar sleeps,
men with boots trace arabesques
on porridge coloured skies.
The Nith is paralysed
and the moon decides to shine again
on lawns, on little children
disappeared.

While Ian Dunbar sleeps,
taxis purr through sleeves of street,
the night has an eggshell innocence,
smooth like baldness
and the clock strains against the weight
of our sweet
fears.

While Ian Dunbar sleeps,
in the little time
it takes for candlelight to pass,
or to sip a glass
from the River Lethe,
there is no need of death,
or tears.

Girls in Blue Afghan Coats

Past the windows of Caw's Bar,
between the Happy Hour signs
framed by beautiful and pitiless wood
and the photographs of drinkers,
their carcinoma frozen on old film,
spill a hundred little blonde girls
dressed in blue afghan coats.
They are dancing through the black
fretwork railings, down the cobbled street,
past Ladbrokes fired by jagged light.
They are spinning down the Wellgate,
their pigtails are a semaphore,
their smiles a strange tongue,
their dreams beyond us.
We shrug and turn away at last,
back into the head-butt of smoke,
as the dinosaurs might once have done,
in half anticipation of that asteroid.

My Mother's Dictionary

The pages curl back from *arcane*
all the way to *chabazite*
and a paper black with anagrams,
epsils, sepisle, sleep is, sleep is.
Some words are marked.
Otherness in bold red pen, *tutelage.*
Near *Spring*
there's a parchment of a leaf.
In the margin by *violin,*
the name *O' Brien,*
mysteriously underlined.
Fanning the pages is to breathe her in,
to the point you can imagine her, *witchcraft,*
by that roaring fire again, smoke curling,
words circling her legs like cats.

Old Photograph

It is VE Night, Tobermory.
Cottages blaze and shimmer in the mirror of the bay.
Light is necklaced everywhere,
on the cross-trees of destroyers,
on the hulls of every cockleshell and scalloper afloat,
even on the gutted snout of a U-Boat,
but there are shadows, to imagine
the black and frozen water
and the land, lonely of men,
from Sunart to Mers-el-Kébir.

Daisy chained by sailors, three WAAFS
pose for a photograph.
Her friends are grinning, wide-eyed,
but my mother's smile is dying
and she's turned away
to the sound of the waves,
as if she could sense my father,
whose war would never cease,
limping inexorably back to her
across the oil-scarred sea.

A Curse on Sister Owens

Picture the scene:
a field hospital in Tripoli,
my father close to pulp.
A nurse, I imagine her

slim, high boned,
an English rose,
is sending back
my mother's note.

"In his present state",
she writes (unruffled by the heat,
I bet, a Prefect of the charnel house)
"I fear this dreadful news

would be too much."
So I have this pious bitch
to thank then

for these winter streets,
and all the afternoons
chasing my reflection
through the puddles of Dumfries.

I have her to praise
for the Sunday League abuse,
the coverings-up and making do,
Ayrshire gulag holidays

and bug-eyed Aunts,
hidden treasuries of guilt,
and the sense that anything
half good can't last,

for the apocalypse of genes
that Sister Owens arranged,
all my disasters in waiting.

Sometimes I dream of my Free French father,
last spotted, they think, in a photo,
sleeping by his Spitfire.
Behind him slow clouds unroll

over hop fields.
He got through the Summer's
dangers unscathed,
with his scarf and labrador.

I have seen him since, in magazines
and café society.
He is a philosopher, or novelist.
He has lovers and wives.

He is golden. The sun is everywhere:
on his face, his hair,
the place not taken.

On the Coast of North West England

Willowherb through ribs of iron fret
and red flowers of rust.
Grey houses scattered by the wind

root grimly, bud
blunt kids, skimming stones on sad beaches
thinking of America,

and the arcades at the end of the world.
Dregg, Flimby, Netherton,
in the armpits of dead factories,

their curtains closed
as the sea lies limp at their doors,
the fog off shore vague like old nightmares.

In Maryport men from the pubs
lug fish and chips
as the gulls, mimicking their fathers,

follow the little wake home.

After a Storm

Coal dark, pinned through with
the brightest slivers of moon,
stars, twin tailed comet.
After the storm, the ocean is dead;
only lanterns toss
at the memory and, somewhere,
tyres plough water.
What's left of the gale,
mere dry sobbing,
brings the scent of wild garlic.
I lean back, the half broken spars
sharp in my ribs,
and look, past fingers of carob
and your sleeping shape,
to the flattest union of sea and sky.

Marked

Linn McGarr,
I am marking your exam in the bar.
It's a highly unethical thing:
my own experience confirms
that ten pints can leave in tatters
the critical apparatus.

I have no choice, Linn McGarr.
I have taken on a thousand papers
so that myself and Jane
can go on our honeymoon to Spain.
I have to mark them constantly,
on the bus, at the toilet, in my sleep.
It is a hard and desperate life, Mc G,
I suspect you would concur with me.

And the pub is not so bad.
Summer stabs
through little slats of window,
corkscrews of dust glow,
dance in their spotlights,
rich gantry green and ambers ignite.
Are you in the sun, Linn McGarr?
Is it sparking concretes in Craigmillar?

I see, Linn McGarr,
you think Asquith was murdered
by Emily Pankhurst in 1903.
After another pint I am tempted to agree
(his later photographs show a corpse-like pallor)
and Trotsky, you say, overthrew Stalin.
Credit will always be given
to valid pieces of wishful thinking,

and your response to the Triple Entente,
"Who cares?" seems sublime, succinct,
though it's not in the marking scheme,
and I like the way you dot the 'I' in Linn,
like a little bubble hovering in space,
above the mediocrity of name and place.

It is strange how fate has done us in.
If I had my way, Linn,
people like you and I would stride out
on the by-ways of history like giants.
Life has other plans for you, me too perhaps.
In the meantime, for what it's worth, full marks.

Faculty Meeting

We have gathered to consider
our Improvement Plan.
It is important to have one,
though maybe not this afternoon.

Outside, the sun toasts trees,
it is their quality indicator,
streets yawn away for miles
without monitor or review,
a little girl kicks her bag along the road,
oblivious of tracking,
and where is the comparison decile
that can measure the point of this
against any other single thing we'd rather do?

We sit and breathe, and blink,
and purse our lips.
We are alive, and our lives
waft away on balmy drafts
of inconsequence.

Summer in Dumfries

There is a watery summer in Dumfries.
We are sending up clouds of small town
ill feeling to block the sun,
and while we slowly turn
the colour we were before,
our children gleam, white kneed,
on trampolines,
our terriers crap on putting greens,
and the river passes us by,
carrying our bottles and kebab boxes,
filled with messages for other cities,
out to sea.

I am sitting at the 'Mandy Jones
is a hoor' picnic table,
rather than the 'Billy's a fat poof' one,
where there is a huge herring gull
scoffing cold chips.
From here I can see
the deserted ramparts of the crazy golf,
and past languid plumes of trees,
the hard spires of another Dumfries,
not necessarily a better one.

Little mobs of pensioners pass,
a thin girl on a bike,
a man whistling a tune from 'Cats'.
All this is astounding.
While the birds hop assuredly between us,
hunting, gathering,
we are walking in the park wondering
when Safeways shuts,
how, in the absence of something,
we are in Dumfries.

February

Wild Kingholm Quay
on my paternity leave.
I am fighting in the fist of a gale
and even with the eight-wheel
drive caterpillar tracked
ocean-going Mamas and Papas
bank-busting buggy
it's not easy.
Three quarters of the way there,
a classic dilemma:
how to open my bottle of beer
without the baby being blown into the water.
I lash the pram to me with my belt.
No-one can accuse me of selfishness.
This is better than back home
with the Baby Gym by God!
You can mollycoddle kids.
Look, it's snowing.

Primary Numbers

Lydia is one year old today.
She does not know the tyranny

of numbers. Some teacher,
eye half-hung on a farmer,

will start her accounting.
Now, there is just one of everything:

one cat, that's something big and grazes,
one dog in hundreds of disguises,

one tree repeatedly gone past,
one bed, one breakfast,

one howling rhapsody
to celebrate every day.

Myself, I regret a singularity of fate.
There are no more multiples of forty eight.

Out of the Way

Lydia has pink sandals
and butterfly clips:
it's sunny in the gardens,
the grass tiger stripes,

the news only a distant wheeze
from a kitchen radio,
drowned by bees,
a breeze, the birdsong.

This is why we're here:
nothing to worry over
but tumbles on soft lawns,
that and the vicious roar

of fighter bombers, spinning
like needles over garden sheds,
practising pitching bombs
on babies' heads.

Points Missed

Lydia has found a star in the park,
among the wood and cinders.
She cups it in her hands:
What will we do, Daddy?
I smile absent-mindedly down.
Jump up, she shouts, and throw it back.

I am wondering whether
it will ever be summer,
if the money can last,
if my current aches will kill me,
while Lydia roots in the here and now,

and turns up star after star after star.

from *Strange Bamboo*, 2007

My Father

Fathers were good to my pals
lectured them about cash
then bought them flats,
deplored their morals

but flitted them from place to place
at dead of night.
Oh my Dad'll go spare
they'd cheerfully admit

as they phoned for loans.
At such times
I would remember my own
and his two pieces of advice:

how to remove your bayonet
from an enemy's ribcage,
and how to disarm a maniac
coming at you from the stairs.

They thought their fathers weird
for having cardigans,
I thought mine odd
because he'd talk to men

who'd burned alive in 1942
and because of other things
I'd watched him do:
vault walls three times his size,

or sprint along a busy street
to punch my Mum. When he went,
it left a hole as a trepan might.
I have no idea where he ended up

though I knew he would live long,
as mad folk do.
Years down the line
I received a sentence or two,

written in his cramped
and delicate monkish way,
I wonder, it began,
if you remember me...

Rabbit Rovers' Last Game

You'll not remember season 94 to 95:
You were about eight,
and the cup final was a thriller.
The crowd was on its feet,

all furry animals, steeped in the hype
and the history of the game.
My team, all slightly shady types,
lost in extra time,

a volley from that poacher Ralph the Dog
that Ivan Squirrel couldn't grasp.
Then the score was duly logged
and filed with all the other stats,

the stars lined up for autographs,
as the fans were gathered up to go,
and you headed thoughtfully for your bath
none of us to know

the goalposts were about to shift,
the boot stuck in by nature,
and even Ivan with his giant palms
couldn't keep out the future.

August

to Andrea & Grievy

Summer in the town.
The rain is solid,
you can see tall trees drowning in it,
roads like tongues vomiting it out.
Lydia and I, dressed for Malibu,
are stuck in a bus shelter,
listening to its corrugated tattoo,
and the howl of cars bent on fat puddles.
It's a minimalist structure,
no comfort to be given to the frail,
or the knackered,
only concrete and flaking paint
and a family of leaks.
The thing about here, though,
is that Andrea loved Grievy in 1993.
It is written huge,
repeatedly, in many styles,
in the middle of walls,
the corners, and in patterns like
webs leaking from the roof tiles,
and we are suddenly warmed, the baby and I,
to know that ten years ago, love was born here
strong enough to stencil,
to painstakingly colour,

to shade in different felt pens,
as the endlessly knuckle- headed world
caroomed past, oblivious as ever
to the small miracles that make it worth
a damn.

September

Lydia says I should drink cider,
not red wine today –
it stains the teeth. I always obey
the baby in such matters

and just as well. I'm slowly drinking up
when, out of the ether, you arrive.
As usual, I'm surprised
there's no actual thunderclap,

no heavily spiced breeze from the Levant,
no flunkies actively engaged
to shovel all plump bastards beyond range
of your sudden smile, your heron's laugh,

and, as always, I get a fright
from my own internal calypso,
as if things weren't done and dusted long ago.
We talk, while sunlight

plays on your lap like kittens
and when you're gone
and the whole room drained of colour, oxygen,
I'm still grinning.

Outside, clouds are strangling the day.
Looks like drizzle says the baby.
She puts on her Mary Poppins face:
back to wine, I'd say.

A Poet Sitting Under a Wall Mistakes Some Pints of Magners for the Muse

The baby's woken up
just in time to save me from a poem
that was about to feature a 'filigree of cloud'
and 'scrimshaw against the sky'.
Scrimshaw is the last resort,
so thank God:
it is a mercy killing.
Now I will focus on mixing milk
and watching the hills
march across the horizon
like the front cover of The People's Friend.

The Lost Poems

I have come back to Mull
for the poems that were lost here;
overboard from the Lochinvar,
buried in landslips,
left in telephone boxes,
torn to pieces and
somersaulting in the wind.
I am in sore need of them now,
for they were born of bright agonies
before they slipped away:
death, love, betrayal.
All these years
they have been dancing on the shore
perfect as little fawns.
I will set foot on Mull tonight
and they will be waiting for me
by the tree-line at twilight,
wearing the faces I had,
dark, fine and hard.

First Day Back

We sit and wait to be addressed,
we with desperate tans
or brand new heads
after surgery in Surinam,
but there is no escape...

"You have no comfort zone", they say,
and smile and stroke their palms
with the easy grace of folk on 60 grand,
no kids to face.
"There is no breathing space..."

Another time another place they'd be alright,
they could be gardeners,
or air-hostesses, simple types
and nice, but they have garnered
grim epiphanies.

Some council fools
have said they make some sense,
worse, can make a difference,
and now they have a roost to rule,
and won't let lie.

No comfort zone, and they see
"amazing challenges" ahead.
The Aussie teachers parachuted
here to stiffen spines agree.
They will go over the top at dawn

tomorrow without a care.
The sunlight seems to shine
on every individual head inclined
as if in prayer,
but there is no comfort zone.

The Men from Duncow

On Saturdays men with jackets
too checked to look upon
come down the hills from Duncow,
their hands corrugated or hung
over sticks like old oven gloves.

They are from impenetrable places,
runrig, dyke and quarry,
Rommel and Sicily,
from long lines of lives
stuck in monochrome.

Through drowned chipbags
and crying kids they come,
their talk arcane,
their existence in this
café-bar a mystery.

They sit and soak up whisky
like blotters, until darkness
climbs over rooftops,
then they rise stiffly from the smoke
like metal men,

and the night, and the pub,
close again round
more comfortable themes,
faces flush with puggie light,
alcopops and plasma screens,

for time moves on and that's a fact,
though the men from Duncow clamber back.

March Past

Let us salute the monsters
we created: these men with buckles
and fierce, rheumy eyes,

all that weight on their backs
of fear and hatred
still sharp as a field pack,

these men who lived in hell
and often, later, passed it on,
these men who tremble

when they see a German tourist
or a Jap. How can they expect us
to make sense of it,

these lives in suspension?
They are harder to deal with
than headstones.

Let us just wave and celebrate
with some cant
and mild embarrassment:

they'll be dead next year.

Millennium 2

I'm sitting on Cairnpapple Hill
waiting for the aliens to come
and liberate West Lothian.
I have a probe in my head
they planted years ago:
sometimes it picks up police frequencies.
You know, Jesus was an alien,
you can tell from his ears
and that funny sign he makes with his fingers
like the Klingons.
I think when the aliens come
West Lothian will be a better place,
though maybe not for cows:
I don't know why they turn them inside out.
They'll build pyramids
and live in Roslin Chapel
with John the Baptist's head.
We'll have the holy grail again
and men will walk abroad in parkas.

Oz Aerobics

Monday: 'Oz Aerobics',
sun blackened girls by Sydney Bridge.
I love the one at the back, with the biggest chest,
she is more awkward than the rest,
but I know her dream –
to be at the front of the screen.

She is seldom in focus,
but when she is,
her smile seems nervous.
It is hard being a health fascist.
Though without a pinch of fat,
she fears for her foothold on the mat.

I wonder if, at night,
she relaxes by lava light,
and watches *Dumfries Drunks* on satellite TV,
and has a sneaking crush for me,
rumpled, plump, on the edge of my stool,
fearful of the back row somewhere, too.

Tam's Room

Surrounded by the guts
of spilled out bags
and ceiling high Sunday supplements,
Tam sleeps,
in the gentle shade of a canopy
of underwear,
and the discarded socks of a tired army.

His room
looks as if it's been beachcombed
by some abandoned mariner,
the glasses, the bright fragments
picked out by light
through sun bleached curtains.

Tam has a spine
of novels at his back,
his baccy,
his bottle of Glengoyne,
but there's a football strip,
boys size it seems,
hanging on the wardrobe's lip,

stirring slightly
like some small memory of sailing
with the tide.

Holiday Cottage, Out of the Way

Lismore, raw as bacon,
and the merest hint of Morvern
under heavy rain.
Daily the sky changes from black
to slightly less than black
and back again.
We pray for greyness;
grey is an exotic dream for us.
Five days ago
the storm stopped for a while,
long enough to dig a hole
between the snotty rows
of dead jellyfish. We watched
it fill with water,
a highlight, looking back.
Every day, with a languid
kind of desperation we visit
orphaned seals, damp alpacas,
the wind chiselled streets of frontier towns,
and everywhere we go, surly girls
in polo shirts and shorts
charge us forty quid.
We don't go out at all
now the baby's crocked,
spend half the night with Calpol,
half pints of malt,
stare out the window at the oily dark
search the seams of nothingness
for a beaten track.

Another Lost Boy on the Cumnock Bus

A little crow in his shiny suit
but he has a voice like something put
on metal to scratch cars,
and a good half inch of Vladivar

left between his knees.
In front, old ladies squeeze
against their seats like paste.
He's not out of his face,

it's just that Big Ted
bounced a brick off his head
the other day,
and now his girlfriend wants his DNA.

He takes a swig. Outside, the valley
where we both were born sways
in shades of green and brilliant yellows.
It's summer and it follows

the plot we've long since lost.
His mobile goes off:
No Da, I'm sober and I'm dressed.
Aye. I really am. Honest.

The little box goes dead.
He sits and gravely nods his head,
then stares quite sadly up at us,
as he lobs his bottle up the bus.

The Man Whose Last Kiss Was Me

1982, Italy had won.
The chants were red throated,
Rossi, Rossi.
As we drank to surrogate victory,
an elephant wandered by,
draped in the tricolour, then,
even stranger,
a young man jumped from his moped,
ran up and kissed me full on the lips,
me, who'd never been kissed by the sun or men.
His mouth smelled of wine.
Then he turned back,
his white shirt flapping,
through closing shadow
and the faces of girls he'd never meet
and was run down and killed.
What an odd contact:
grey Dumfries, tormented by rain,
it's people fat with coats,
and Florence, hammered by sunlight,
it's kids bare kneed,
and one dead
in a spreading halo of black blood,
his taste on my lips still.

from *The Lost Garden*, 2010

Patriotism

(In 1964 the Queen unveiled an equestrian
statue of Robert Bruce overlooking the field at
Bannockburn.)

When I first saw Bruce, scooped shining
from bronze in a blade of autumn sun,
he had the jaw of a superhero,
gaze fixed on the cartoon world in peril,
Dr Octopus in Stirling Castle,
or the Circus of Doom crossing the Bannock Burn.
Too remote to be real:
my father was mashed in war and I was not
of a generation to think anywhere,
least of all Scotland, that grey puddled place
shut on a Sunday, worth dying for.

As long as it was for something prefixed
'international' I marched across the land,
until, when finally standing still,
my country grew uninvited round me,
not the one with heroes shrunk the size
of shortbread tins, or even a sweep of landscape
that takes the breath like a blow in the gut,
but the one seen in the boss of a child's eye,
her face sore with smiling,
that Scotland it turns out, a place
worth living for.

George 5th Earl Seton, from the portrait

by Frans Pourbus the Elder

George looks as comfortable
as any old centre half would in a ruff.
He holds his youngest like basketballs
but this is no family huddle.
The older kids scuff about behind:
they resent being ginger
and that their father has hitched
his wagon to another falling star.
Their Ma's at the shops, she thinks
making ends meet on a spy's wages
is hard enough without
paying for fancy portraits.
The Spanish have run rings round George:
the old legs are giving in
and he's staring relegation in the face.
All his hopes are pinned on the wee man,
but he's got a copy of the Dandy
inside that Catechism and thinks
the old faith's dead as Cow Pie.

Rousing Speeches of the Middle Ages as heard by the back row of spearmen

Who would be a tidal wave
and hold their matchwood sheep?
Turn that flea!
but lying in your shed many years from now
you'll feel bratwurst you were not here
and trade all the sleighs between macao and yen
for the chants to say
you can take our wives
but you'll never take our crispins,
wa-hey!

Scorched Earth

Clouds thick as oil over Nithsdale:
the fields are in flame.
In the dark we take our children
and go, like beasts, to the woods,
or north, where the smoke will follow like a dog.
Tomorrow they will find our soil split and curdled,
pregnant with ash, and after a while
they will leave, and we will dream of the harvest,
and the fire that followed the harvest,
and the famine that follows the fire.

Pope Boniface VIII Sums Up the Evidence

*In 1301 in the conflict between King John
Balliol and Edward I of England, both sides
were at great pains to present evidence to the
Papacy to support their positions.*

"We have puzzled over these petitions
Not least because both pursuants
speak the same tongues
and possess many of the same dislikeable attributes...
The testimony of the English Crown
is scholarly, deep in genealogy and law
and drawn from venerable sources beyond repute.
Its argument- that the Scots were but a younger
branch of the tribe that migrated to Britannia
after the Roman conquest- has impressed
the lawyers and historians of the Holy See.
Baldred Bissett on the other hand claims,
with no evidence at all, that the Scots
are descended from a daughter of Pharaoh
who, after a heavy night with some Irish sailors
in Ayia Napa, found herself drifting at sea
and later washed up at Lochgilphead
with a strange stone (which later disappeared),
all this while the Romans- to use his own words-
'were a piss-poor tribe of skanks in mud huts.'
Bissett also claims to have incontrovertible proof of this
but left it in a kebab shop last night in the Piazza Roma..."

Three Letters from a Tenant to MacMhaolain Mor, 1745–46

*The National Trust of Scotland has been
searching for people whose ancestors were
involved in the Jacobite Rebellion 1745–46.*

I

I am sorry I could not come to Moidart.
My youngest has a spot
behind her ear that may be chicken pox
but I have instructed my son Andrew to join you.
He is tall and strong as a deer and is studying
Geography
and Politics at Dundee University.
He will wash our sword many times in English blood.

II

I am sorry I missed the rout at Falkirk.
It is virtually impossible to get a bus from here
outwith the tourist season,
and my son had an interview with Patientline,
but we have the fire of Fingal in our veins
and will join you
when the summer timetables begin.

III

I am sorry to have missed you at Culloden
but I had an apex ticket and had to return
or pay a heavy supplement.
Exile is hell. My heart bleeds in this Travelodge.
Andrew begs your indulgence as well:
he thought Carrbridge was Cambridge
and stayed on for the Folk Festival.

Proof At Last

It's in the rock record,
but we could have guessed.
Years ago, balmy Scotland
hugged the equator,
golden beaches, lush forests,
coconuts, bars on stilts,
beach volleyball, then one day
earth's orbit tipped to an ellipse,
plates shifted, the oceans shut,
and on that flimsy pretext
England came hurling up
from its place in the Antarctic
and slammed us with its icy spine
into the North Atlantic,
shunted up the sheuch
of Iceland with all the ensuing
mountains, herring, sleet,
Sundays, words like sheuch...
That's it. No need for further talk.
At last, it's proved, it's all their fault.

Lochinver

Lochinver. The end of the track.
Black swallows black
and the storm howls like a dog.
At the quay, in orange fog,
a ship spews out whiskery fish
and you, in Dumfries,
are crackling over the phone
picking at the bones
of my latest lunacy. I nod
but I am really wondering
if this phonebox on its outcrop of scree
can be seen from sea
by that schooner
crewed by dead sailors,
or by aliens circling,
hungry for pineal gland.
Yes I'm sorry, it won't happen again,
and the rain sounds like drums
in this bubble of yellow light,
emptiness everywhere like the tide.

My Feet

Tuesday: the birds softly bugle
end of day. I look at my feet,
bare and wriggling on hot concrete.
They are pitted, spurred, I see,
cracked as white wood.
They are at the business end, my feet,
still dodging, chasing lost causes,
up in the night silent as slippers.
To my head, at the other extreme,
they are mere beasts of burden.
Though they work for the same body
there is no camaraderie there,
no joint sense of mission.
My feet think my head's had it easy,
up there in the fresh air all these years,
talking crap. Where would it be without
them to do the donkey work?
No fancy products wasted on their upkeep,
just soap and water, cheap socks.
I think if my feet ever met my head again
they'd give it a good kicking.

Moonshine

Cold streets washed with moonshine
and the sea hidden, mumbling, below our feet.
Across the Firth the diamond lamps in Fife,
but even through a fog of hops

we sniffed the perfumes of a more exotic land
and gazed from the high windows
of The Old Chain Pier or The Starbank
through darkness to the edge of the world.

Weaving home as the foghorns coughed
we swore to follow the night
to Timbuktu, Nevada, Samarkand.
I only got as far as Greece, holidays with the wife,

but when I last saw you, in Ninewells,
tubed and tightly gauzed in white,
you were still more in than out of the dream,
ready to travel light.

Hamecomin'

In the lee o John Knox's yew
(ane thing o beauty still staunin
at least despite his threapin)
we toss oor cabers as though
it's the naitural thing tae dae after breakfast.
Ower the firth, Dumbarton Rock
is mired in mist, or speerits,
like the braes o Ben Jiggery Pokery
or the gleet in yon American's ee
as he minds the cabers o his forebears
lost in Lochaber lang syne.
The morn we will rake a rickle o stanes,
be blood brithers in a kirk hidit
in the wilds, an toast oor common bonds
in fists o malt, for are we no a mairit
tae the same shooglie territory o mynd,
a nation that is and isnae, as solit
as a sea-loch's soughin,
the mutter o an editorial,
the tingle o tills far off in the gloaming?

Burnsiana

Rab Wilson and Calum Colvin
ISBN: 978-1-910021-01-9
PBK £9.99

Combining art and poetry to form a beautiful new alternative to current Burns related titles, Colvin's photographic artworks go hand-in-hand with Wilson's witty and insightful poetry to provide a daring take on the world of Robert Burns.

Employing the unique fixed-point perspective of the camera, Colvin creates elaborate narratives from manipulated and constructed images so as to comment on aspects of Scottish culture, identity and the human condition in the early 21st Century. Wilson in turn, responds to these images, giving a deeper alternative meaning to the artworks and dwells on who we are, where we have been, and towards what we may become.

Rab Wilson is one of the best poets now working in Scotland. In the interest of his language, subject matter, form of address, development of style and perspective and tone, he is far more curious and willing to take risks than almost all of his contemporaries.
ALAN RIACH

100 Favourite Scottish Poems

Edited by Stewart Conn
ISBN: 978-1-905222-61-2
PBK £7.99

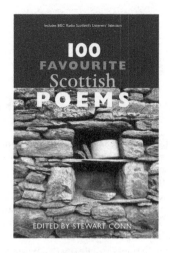

Scotland has a long history of producing outstanding poetry. From the humblest but-and-ben to the grandest castle, the nation has a great tradition of celebration and commemoration through poetry. *100 Favourite Scottish Poems* – incorporating the top 20 best-loved poems as selected by a BBC Radio Scotland listener poll – ranges from ballads to Burns and from 'Cuddle Doon' to 'The Jeelie Piece Song'.

Edited by Stewart Conn, poet and inaugural recipient of the Institute of Contemporary Scotland's Iain Crichton Smith Award for services to literature (2006). Published in association with the Scottish Poetry Library.

Luath Press Limited
committed to publishing well written books worth reading

LUATH PRESS takes its name from Robert Burns, whose little collie Luath (*Gael.*, swift or nimble) tripped up Jean Armour at a wedding and gave him the chance to speak to the woman who was to be his wife and the abiding love of his life. Burns called one of 'The Twa Dogs' Luath after Cuchullin's hunting dog in Ossian's *Fingal*. Luath Press was established in 1981 in the heart of Burns country, and now resides a few steps up the road from Burns' first lodgings on Edinburgh's Royal Mile. Luath offers you distinctive writing with a hint of unexpected pleasures.

Most bookshops in the UK, the US, Canada, Australia, New Zealand and parts of Europe either carry our books in stock or can order them for you. To order direct from us, please send a £sterling cheque, postal order, international money order or your credit card details (number, address of cardholder and expiry date) to us at the address below. Please add post and packing as follows: UK – £1.00 per delivery address; overseas surface mail – £2.50 per delivery address; overseas airmail – £3.50 for the first book to each delivery address, plus £1.00 for each additional book by airmail to the same address. If your order is a gift, we will happily enclose your card or message at no extra charge.

Luath Press Limited
543/2 Castlehill
The Royal Mile
Edinburgh EH1 2ND
Scotland
Telephone: 0131 225 4326 (24 hours)
email: sales@luath.co.uk
Website: www.luath.co.uk